JASMINE AND JINNS

An Amaltas tree in full bloom in Delhi summer
Photo: Rachit Dhawan

JASMINE AND JINNS

Memories and Recipes of My Delhi

SADIA DEHLVI

Photographs
Omar Adam Khan

HarperCollins *Publishers* India

First published in India 2017 by
HarperCollins *Publishers* India

P-ISBN: 978-93-5264-436-0
E-ISBN: 978-93-5264-437-7

2 4 6 8 10 9 7 5 3 1

Sadia Dehlvi asserts the moral right
to be identified as the author of this work.

The views and opinions expressed in this book
are the author's own and the facts are as reported by her,
and the publishers are not in any way liable for the same.

Photographs : Omar Adam Khan

HarperCollins *Publishers*
A-75, Sector 57, Noida, Uttar Pradesh 201301, India
1 London Bridge Street, London, SE1 9GF, United Kingdom
2 Bloor Street East, Toronto, Ontario M4W 1A8, Canada
Lvl 13, 201 Elizabeth Street (PO Box A565, NSW, 1235), Sydney NSW 2000, Australia
195 Broadway, New York, NY 10007, USA

Typeset in 12/15 Bembo Std
by Jojy Philip, New Delhi

Printed and bound at
Thomson Press (India) Ltd

For
Amma, Abba, Nani, Daddy, Ammi, Apa Saeeda, Mamoo Abdullah
and my extended Dehlvi family
and all those for whom 'Dehli' is a way of life

Photo: Mayank Austen Soofi

Contents

An iftaar at the dargah of Hazrat Nizamuddin Auliya

In the name of Allah Most Merciful Most Compassionate

The best amongst you are those who feed others
and offer greetings of peace to those whom you know and
those whom you do not know.

Prophet Muhammad ﷺ

Gratitude

Traditionally, family recipes were never shared with outsiders but just passed on from mother to daughter. Some of my aunts took offence on being asked for recipes. Decades ago, I remember a guest insisting that my aunt tell her the recipe of the nihari she had served. Avoiding the request, she offered to send the family the preparation whenever they wished. The lady remained adamant, saying it would not be right to impose frequent requests. Reluctantly, my aunt gave the recipe, which the lady hurriedly noted. After the visitor left, I expressed surprise at her large heartedness. With a mischievous smile she retorted, 'I am not so foolish. I did not reveal one main ingredient! She can never make it taste the way I prepare nihari.'

Withholding a key ingredient is a standard trick deployed by many women and professional cooks. In yesteryears, a woman's worth was pretty much valued by housekeeping skills, and cooking played a large role. When the menfolk went to work, women's lives revolved around the kitchen.

Initially, I anticipated problems in getting my aunts to share their cooking secrets. Instead, I found them willing and excited. Age has caught up with them and some are no longer around. Fortunately, they have passed on their culinary secrets to their daughters, and some to their daughters-in-law. Given the modern sharing culture, the younger lot happily gave me some of these recipes.

I had a wonderful time writing this book as it connected me to relatives whom otherwise one meets mostly at family weddings and funerals. I enjoyed visiting the homes of aunts and cousins, and they all fed me their delicious specialties.

Jalebi: A popular Indian sweet

I am particularly grateful to my amazing cousins Qurratulain, Farah, Asiya and my aunts Khala Rabia and Choti Auntie Ameena for helping me with recipes over the years. When cooking something that I wasn't confident about, I sought their advice. God bless the souls of Amma, Abba, Nani, Mamoo Abdullah and Apa Saeeda, from whom I learnt much more than just about food. I remain indebted to Ammi, my mother, for her constant criticism and I hope someday she approves of my cooking! I am sharing these recipes as an effort to preserve my 'Dehli' that is fading away.

I cooked all the recipe dishes which were photographed at home. Apart from the goolar, kachnar bharta and sangri salan, which I made for the first time, all other dishes are cooked regularly in my kitchen. I hope you try these recipes and that they bring cheer to your table.

All the new photos unless specified otherwise have been taken by Omar Adam Khan. I thank him for these wonderful photographs that make this book as much his as mine. Thank you Sidrah Fatma Ahmed for helping with all the photo shoots.

I thank Vaseem, my brother, and Himani, my sister-in-law, for their indulgence and support. Immense gratitude to Mayank Austen Soofi, the official taster at home, for his suggestions at various stages of the manuscript. Thank you Jojy for typesetting all my books and helping design the pages. I thank Shreya Punj of HarperCollins for her dedication. Thank you Shaaz for your tireless efforts in creating the cover. I remain grateful to Karthika V.K. for accompanying me on my journey as an author. From the depths of my heart, I thank all those who bless my table by sharing meals at my home.

Khari Baoli Spice Market in Delhi

A Slice of the Past

Little is known about Delhi's food culture before the arrival of the Delhi sultans in the twelfth century. These sultans belonged to warrior clans of Central Asia, where food was more about survival than sophistication. The refinement in their cuisine came through interactions with local Indian communities and the abundance of fruits, vegetables and spices available here. The tables of Qutubuddin Aibak, Iltutmish and Razia Sultan consisted of meat dishes, dairy products, fresh fruits and varieties of local vegetables.

The fourteenth-century poet and historian Amir Khusrau wrote of the tables of Sultan Muhammad bin Tughlaq which consisted of about 200 dishes. The royal kitchen fed about 20,000 people daily. In his famous Persian Mathnawi *Qiran us Sa'dain*, the epic poem that later came to be known as *Mathnavi dar Sifat-e-Dehli* for its glorification of Delhi's culture, Khusrau writes, 'The royal feast included sharbet labgir, naan-e-tanuri, sambusak, pulao and halwa. They drank wine and ate tambul after dinner.' He describes the addition of two varieties of bread, naan-e-tunuk, a lighter bread, and naan-e-tanuri, bread baked in a tandoor. In addition, Khusrau mentions delicacies such as sparrow and quail, along with a variety of sharbet made from roses, pomegranates, oranges, mangoes and lemons.

In the *Travels of Ibn Battuta in Asia and Africa*, translated by Gibb, Ibn Battuta describes a royal meal at the table of the early fourteenth century Sultan Ghiyasuddin at Tughlaqabad as a lavish spread comprising 'thin round bread cakes; large slabs of sheep mutton; round dough cakes made with ghee and stuffed with almond paste and honey; meat cooked with onions and ginger; sambusak that

1

Spices and dry fruits in Khari Baoli, Delhi

were triangular pasties made of hashed meat with almonds, walnuts, pistachios, onions, and spices placed inside a piece of thin bread fried in ghee, much like the samosa of today; rice with chicken topping; sweet cakes and sweetmeat for dessert.'

Ibn Battuta mentions sharbet of rose water that was served before meals, which ended with paan. He writes of mangoes, pickled green ginger and peppers; jackfruit and barki, a yellow gourd with sweet pods and kernels; sweet oranges; wheat, chickpeas, lentils and rice. Sesame and sugarcane were also cultivated. He describes Indians eating millet, especially pounded millet made into a porridge cooked with buffalo milk. Peas and moong dal cooked with rice and ghee were served for breakfast. Animals were fed barley, chickpeas, leaves as fodder and were even given ghee.

The arrival of the Mughals in the sixteenth century added aroma and colour to Delhi's culinary range. Although Babur, the founder of the Mughal dynasty, had little time for Indian food. In *Baburnama*, his memoirs, the emperor complains about the lack of muskmelons, grapes and other fruits plentiful in his Afghan homeland. Babur's son and successor Emperor Humayun is credited with bringing refined Persian influences to Delhi's cuisine. This resulted from his years spent in Persia after having been defeated by Sher Shah Suri. The fusion of Indian and Persian styles of cooking came to be known as 'Mughal cuisine'.

In *Ain-i-Akbari*, Abul Fazal, Emperor Akbar's courtier, mentions that cooks from Persia and various parts of India were part of the royal kitchen. This led to the merging of Turkish, Afghan, Indian and Persian ways of cooking. Fazal chronicles that more than 400 cooks from Persia formed the large kitchen establishment that had head cooks, official tasters and numerous administrative departments.

He writes about rice from different regions, duck and waterfowl from Kashmir and special breeds of chicken raised for banquets, handfed with pellets flavoured with saffron and rosewater. Beef was rarely eaten, and pork was forbidden. A kitchen orchard and garden supplied fresh vegetables and fruits such as lemons, pomegranates, plums and melons. Many dry fruits, including almonds, were cultivated. A typical meal consisted of dozens of dishes made from grains, vegetables, rice, goat, chicken and fowl. Indian delicacies such as poori, khandwi and daal-kachori became part of the royal table. In addition to these accounts, *Ain-i-Akbari* contains the ingredients and ways of preparing various types of halwa, pulao, kebab, meat and vegetables.

During the rule of Emperor Shah Jahan in the seventeenth century, the Mughal Empire reached its zenith. Exquisite architecture, extravagance and luxury came to define Delhi's royal court. The cooks continued to be trained in Persian, Indian and Afghan methods. Despite political decline in later centuries, the Mughals maintained their lavish lifestyles. The indulgent tables of the last Mughal Emperor Bahadur Shah Zafar are legendary. The Mughals faded away, but left Delhi with a cuisine that remains an integral part of the city's cultural heritge.

Red chillies were brought to India by the Portuguese who began its cultivation in Goa during the sixteenth century. Two hundred years later, red chillies made their way to Delhi.

Shah Jahan's daughter, Princess Jehanara laid out Chandni Chowk, which acquired the reputation of one of the world's best bazaars. A canal flowed through it, beautifying the area and providing the city with an accessible water body. During the reign of the Mughal Emperor Muhammed Shah Rangeela in the eighteenth century, the canal's water became polluted. The royal hakims advised the citizens of Delhi to eat chillies to help purge toxins from the body. This eventually led to the inclusion of red chillies in Delhi's food. The romance with chillies created Delhi's famous chaats such as paani ke batashe, papri, chaat pakori, qalmi badey, samosa and kachori.

The cuisine of Shahjahanabad, the walled city which is now called Purani Dilli, has traditionally consisted of both non-vegetarian and vegetarian food. The Muslims and Kayasthas relished meat-based dishes. The Banias and Jains of the city were strict vegetarians, their food free from onion and garlic.

During the Mughal and British period, Banias and Jains were mainly moneylenders, working in the finance departments of the royal court. Khazanchi Wali Gali continues to be known by the residential haveli of the Jain treasurer of Emperor Shah Jahan. Hindus and Muslims both contributed to Delhi's composite culture. Hindu areas were called wara, such as Maliwara and Jogiwara. Muslim areas were mostly called walan, such as Chooriwalan, Suiwalan and Charkhawalan. Mohallas were usually named after the goods sold or manufactured in them.

A large number of the Kayastha community worked in the Mughal courts as record keepers and administrators. Kayastha cuisine became influenced by the Mughal table spread. A variety of traditional Kayastha dishes are made with mutton. Many women from this community did not eat meat, but cooked it in their homes for the menfolk.

Kayasthas are known for their love of good food. Some of their signature dishes are bharva pasanda, ajwain arvi, khadey masaley ka gosht and bhuna gosht. The Kayasthas of Delhi would say in jest, '*Hum parindon main patang aur chaarpai ke alava har chaar pai waali cheez khaate hain,*' barring paper kites we eat everything that flies and apart from the wooden four-legged cot, we eat everything with four legs.

In the old days, Kayasthas did not appear to limit themselves by religious dietary restrictions. During Mughal rule, the community largely lived in the old city. When the British took control of Delhi and moved their administrative quarters to Civil Lines, many Kayastha families shifted to spacious bungalows in this new colony.

The British brought their dietary influences of tea, bread, egg and toast for breakfast, roast chicken, soup and the all-time favourite caramel custard. Delhi's elite adopted some of these English food habits while retaining most of their traditional cuisine. After the Partition in 1947, when the Punjabi immigrants made Delhi their home, the city's culinary ethos changed considerably.

Inside Jama Masjid, Delhi
Photo: Vaseem Ahmed Dehlvi

An Ancestral Journey

A few years ago, I travelled by the comfortable Daewoo Express bus service from Lahore to Islamabad. The bus stopped midway at Bhera for a short break. On seeing the signboard, I became overwhelmed with emotion, got off the bus and touched the ground. My Saraiki-speaking ancestors hailed from Bhera before they migrated to Delhi.

I grew up on stories of my community that calls itself 'Qaum Punjabian'. A community of merchants, we are commonly referred to as 'Dehli Saudagaran'. Given our long association with the city, Abba, my paternal grandfather, adopted 'Dehlvi' as the family name. It simply means 'one from Delhi'. The old *shurufa*, nobility, pronounce Delhi as 'Dehli' in chaste Urdu although 'Dilli' is commonly used.

Family legends tell this story set in the mid-thirteenth century. Families of our biradari, community, were spread over Bhera, Khoshab, Chinot and Sargodha in Punjab. Khatri caste Hindus, they excelled in trade. Once, a group of elders from the biradari headed for a dip in the sacred Ganga river. Somewhere along the way, they encountered the famous Sufi from Afghanistan, Hazrat Shamsuddin Sabswari. He miraculously made them see the Ganga right before their eyes. The whole community embraced Islam at the hands of Hazrat Shamsuddin. His dargah is in Multan, where the tombstone says he died in the year 1276.

To honour Hazrat Shamsuddin, many families added Shamsi to their name. In Moradabad and a few other cities of Uttar Pradesh we are also known as the Shamsi Biradari. On becoming Muslims, the Ahluwalias began to call themselves Allahwalas and the Bahris became Baadis. Some families like the Mehndirattas, Kathurias, Chandnas, Chawlas and Chabras retained their Hindu surnames. Most just dropped their surnames and came to be known by their professions or products they sold. The community has Khilonewaley, Cigarettewaley, Teenwaley, Ghadiwaley, Lacewaley, Chatriwaley, Chashmewaley and many other waleys. My family is called Shamawaley, after the Urdu magazine we published.

Eventually assimilating with the local culture, Urdu became the language of the Saudagaran community. However, some colloquial expressions and words like *pinda*, *nukkad* and *hawka* from the old Saraiki vocabulary are still in use.

It is believed that our community was invited to Delhi by Emperor Shah Jahan on the advice of his *wazir,* prime minister, Saadullah Khan, who came from Chiniot. His family belonged to the Saudagaran biradari and he was aware of their expertise in trade. A plague had ravaged Delhi in 1656, destroying half its population. Shah Jahan wanted to revive the economic life of the city. His minister offered official assurances and privileges to the community, which they accepted. Led by Saadullah Khan in 1657, a caravan of about 350 people including men, women and children arrived in Shahjahanabad – Delhi's seventh city.

Resistant to change and extremely particular about safeguarding their traditions, the Saudagaran migrated along with their *dom*, men who carried invitations from one home to another, and *domni,* professional women who sang at festivals and weddings. They also brought with them their *jarrah*, men who did circumcision and nursed small wounds, *nai* and *nayan*, barbers and matchmakers. Most importantly they migrated with their *khansaama*, professional cooks!

On their arrival in Delhi, Shah Jahan allotted the Saudagaran a piece of land near Kauriya Pul, where the British later built the Dufferin Bridge. This area was once known as Punjabi Katra. In later centuries, a few families moved to Kanpur, Agra, Bareilly, Lucknow, Moradabad and Kolkata. However, most stayed on in Delhi. A prosperous city, it presented countless business opportunities. The Saudagaran did economically well through the centuries and their trading skills earned them the title *Malik ut Taajar*, Kings of Trade.

There is a story that once Bahadur Shah Zafar took ill and

required rare herbs prescribed by the royal hakim. When the herbs were nowhere to be found, someone informed the emperor that the Saudagaran might have them. Senior state officials visited the community elders and the herbs were provided. The emperor recovered from his illness and expressed his desire to reward the community. The Saudagaran did not want money, they asked for three concessions from the royal court. These were granted to them.

The first concession was that the state judiciary would refrain from interfering in their family disputes. To this day, family disputes rarely go to the civil courts and are settled through arbitration of respected community members. The second concession prohibited the police from entering their homes. The third grant allowed the community to keep their dom and domni in their mohallas.

Wedding celebrations in the community usually began at least two weeks prior to the actual marriage ceremony. The domni sang and entertained guests, sitting between the *dehleez*, threshold, of the home and the *gali*, lane, an area called *devdi*. Since these women went singing from house to house, they knew all the families. With their knowledge of boys and girls who had reached a marriageable age, these women doubled up as matchmakers.

At the time of the last Mughal emperor, the Saudagaran mohalla extended from Kaudiya Pul to Kashmiri Gate. This area is around where the Delhi railway station stands today.

Following the uprising of 1857, the English occupied Fatehpuri Masjid and Jama Masjid, banning Muslims from praying in them. The mosques were used as stables for the British cavalry. It was said that there was a proposal to turn the mosques into churches. The British sold the Fatehpuri Masjid to Lala Chunnamal, a rich banker from Chandni Chowk. Rumours put this sum as anywhere between ₹20,000 and ₹60,000.

In 1862, Sikander Begum, the ruler of Bhopal, came to Delhi to meet Lord Canning. She convinced the governor general to return

Steps of the Jama Masjid, Delhi
Photo: Vaseem Ahmed Dehlvi

the Jama Masjid to the Muslims. Sikander Begum participated in the cleansing of the mosque and supervised the resumption of prayers. Later, Lala Chunnamal returned the Fatehpuri Masjid to the Muslims. In lieu of this gesture, the British apparently gave Lala Chunnamal four villages around Delhi in Nangloi and Gurgaon.

As punishment for the 1857 uprising, the English had deprived Delhi of a railway station. Trains bypassed Delhi, the closest station to the city being Ghaziabad. Seemingly forgiving Delhi's citizens for their active participation in the uprising, the station began to be built near Chandni Chowk. Finally, it became operational in 1864 with a single broad gauge train from Calcutta. The residential areas near the station, including the Saudagaran mohalla, were destroyed in the process.

Ballimaran, a mohalla close to Chandni Chowk, got its name from the wooden *balli*, poles, that were made here for use in the construction of the Red Fort and Jama Masjid. It had been home to the Muslim nobility, many of whom were massacred by British forces following the uprising. When their havelis were sold, most of these were bought by members of our community. These included Haveli Hissamuddin Haider, Mahal Serai, Ahata Kaley Sahab and Baradari Nawab Wazir. Restoring some of the old structures, the Saudagaran made their homes in these mohallas. A large wooden *phatak*, gate, was put at the entrance of each mohalla. Those living in Beriwala Bagh, Sheedipura and other outskirt areas shifted to mohallas such as Phatak Habash Khan.

Having moved closer to the centre of town, community members brought shops in Sadar Bazaar. Before Partition, almost all shops in Sadar Bazaar were owned by the Saudagaran. They had a monopoly over the wholesale trade in the city. Many families lived in Mohalla Kishanganj, near Baada Hindu Rao and close to Sadar Bazaar.

Hindu Rao, a wealthy noble, had a *baada*, cattle yard, known as Baada Hindu Rao. The Saudagaran bought the baada and the neighbouring small gardens called Baghichi Acha Jee and Baghichi Ishwari Prasad and built their homes there. In the same vicinity, they also bought a bungalow from a slender, dark and eccentric Anglo-Indian lady who was nicknamed Chuhiya Mem by the residents. The building continues to be called '*Kothi Chuhiya Mem*'.

Several Saudagaran families still live inside these gated mohallas. The increasing congestion, traffic and pollution have led many to move to New Delhi. During the Partition, almost half the number of families migrated to Pakistan. Most of these settled in Karachi, where they have excelled in manufacturing and trade. In Pakistan, they continue to be called 'Dehli Saudagaran'. As of now in India, there are about 8,000 of us in Delhi, with about another 40,000 community members spread across Kolkata, Kanpur, Moradabad and some other cities.

A closely-knit community, the interaction between families remains constant. In the mohallas, the news of deaths and weddings were earlier conveyed by the *chowkidar*, gatekeeper, who went from door to door. Despite many families having moved out, deaths of community members and funeral timings are still announced in the mohallas. This tradition is called *hawka lagvana*. Nowadays, masjid loudspeakers are used for this purpose.

Saudagaran families continued to prosper in Delhi through the twentieth century. Business accounts were kept in *baikhata*, large leather bound registers. These were written in a unique language that was a mix of Saraiki, Hindi and Urdu. No one from outside the community could decipher it. The community had their own *munshi,* accountants. Education imparted to the boys of the community remained basic, with the focus on acquiring business acumen.

Women were mostly confined to their homes and strict purdah was observed. Shopkeepers came home to sell jewellery, clothes, and other such requirements for the women. These were shown to them from behind a curtain or by the men of the house. There was a *mardana*, a designated area in the house for men to entertain their male guests. Only close male relatives were allowed in the *zenana*, women's quarters. Even hawkers were not allowed in our mohallas, other than when the men were home. Except in the immediate neighbourhood, women ventured out in a *doli*, palanquins lifted by four men, who were called *kahar*. Wealthy families kept a *bughie*, horse carriage, in which the curtains were drawn to conceal the women travelling in them.

On reaching puberty, male children were handed over to fellow community members for apprenticeship in business. They were not paid for work as the exercise was aimed at acquiring experience. After this training, boys joined their family business. Men were discouraged from having active social lives outside the community. Government and private jobs were disapproved of, for as public servants they would still be *naukar*, servants, even if it be for the government.

Girls and boys were generally married at a young age. Marriages took place strictly within the community, often amongst first cousins. These customs continue to the present day.

The signs of a thorough gentleman in those days were that his life revolved around *ghar, masjid aur dukaan*, home, mosque and workplace. Girls learnt to read the Quran and were trained in domestic skills. They were brought up to be *dabi dabai,* docile and submissive, so that they would make good wives. Once upon a time, it was said that if girls learned to write, they would begin writing love letters to boys! The thought of girls studying *jughrafia*, geography, was even more terrifying as they could discover ways of running away from home.

Women were taught just enough Urdu to enable them to sign their names on property deeds. Saudagaran families made large property investments. Apart from trade and property, money was generously spent on weddings and food.

Mamoo Abdullah   Mamoo Ilyas and I

Lifestyles of the Saudagaran and other Dilliwalas largely revolved around food. Girls were taught culinary skills before marriage. Women who were not well versed in the art of cooking were perceived as careless homemakers and it was presumed that their men would go astray. I often heard the refrain, '*Aadmi ko pet ke zariye jeeta jata hai,*' men's hearts are won through their bellies.

Punjabi Paranoia

Mamoo Abdullah, my mother's older brother, happened to be a fascinating storyteller. He spent most of his time in libraries and walking around the city. I learnt much about Delhi and family histories from him. His sharp intellect and wit made him everyone's favourite uncle. Seeing all the kids hang around him, Mamoo Ilyas, his older brother, gave him the title 'Commander of the Picnic Empire'.

A witness to the tragedy of the Partition, Mamoo Abdullah saw the Punjabi *sharanarthi, refugees,* as they were then called, rebuild their lives in Delhi. In echoing the response of most Dilliwalas, he often blamed them for eroding the city's language, food and culture. Ammi, my mother, too, remained paranoid about these influences on our lives. Phrases picked up from my Punjabi friends such as '*Mai ney bola*' resulted in immediate admonishment. The elders would say, '*Insaan kehtey hain, janwar boltey hain*'; subtleties of Urdu that are difficult to translate.

If I said, '*Dupatta dal liya,*' Ammi would say, '*Dupatta odha jata hai. Kapda sirf murdey par dala jata hai,*' meaning that you drape a scarf and cover a corpse! When referring to food kept in the fridge or kitchen we could not use the Punjabi expression, '*Khana pada hai.*' Food commanded respect, and the correct way to refer to it was '*Khana rakha hua hai.*' Looking back, the paranoia about Punjabi culture taking over seems rather exaggerated.

Even today, when my mother attends parties at my home and finds the food short of perfection, she invariably comments, '*Tumhare Punjabi doston ke liye theek hai, lekin main jaanti hoon ke behtar ho sakta tha*'. For Ammi, anyone not from Delhi is a Punjabi. Ammi then explains in detail what she found lacking in my cooking. The criticism ranges from less salt, lack of chilli powder or too much garlic. Ammi remains hardest to please, and I am perpetually scared of her scrutiny.

One of the oldest shops that sells savouries on Chandni Chowk, Delhi

Mamoo Abdullah on his part remembered Delhi as the leisurely city, one in which shopkeepers pulled their shutters down to celebrate the monsoon rains. He thought the marketing skills of the Punjabis to be harsh, unlike the softer tones of the Dilliwalas. Mamoo often said, 'Walk through Chandni Chowk and you can tell the difference between an old Dilliwala shopkeeper, Muslim, Hindu, Jain or whatever and a Punjabi migrant shopkeeper. Dilliwalas never beckon you to their shops from the street and do not haggle about prices. They consider such behaviour improper and remain content to sit back and wait for customers.' Once Mamoo made me conscious of this difference, I found that it still holds true.

The original Dilliwalas found it difficult to appreciate the dynamism of the Punjabis during early interactions. They prided themselves on making time to enjoy the finer aspects of life and simply couldn't comprehend those who did not. Eventually, they had to give up their leisurely lifestyles to compete with the hardworking Punjabis.

Daalbiji from Kanwarji's

Kadhai milk being sold in the streets of Matia Mahal in the old city.

The Mystique of Shanjahanabad

Once upon a time, the markets of the old city had a carnival-like atmosphere. Hawkers came up with ingenious ways of grabbing customer attention. Cart vendors selling cucumbers called out, '*Laila ki ungliyaan, Majnu ki pasliyaan, khaao taazi kakdiyaan*,' Laila's fingers and Majnu's ribs, eat fresh cucumbers. Those selling digestive tablets repeated, '*Lakad hazam, pathhar hazam*,' digest wood and stone.

Mamoo told us about dastangoi, the story-telling traditions of the city. In the evenings people gathered around the *dastango*, the storyteller, on the steps of the Jama Masjid. After listening to the riveting stories of conquest, romance, jinns, flying carpets and magic, they enjoyed freshly barbecued kebab. Masita Kebabi was one of Delhi's legendary kebabwalas. One can still relish some of the finest kebab and tikka in the old city.

On festive occasions, affluent families barbecued whole *dumba*, hill goats from Khorasan in Afghanistan. This was common till their disappearance in the late forties. Dumba, with their high proportion of fat, needed no cooking oil and the aroma of the melted fat was supposedly addictive.

I looked forward to visiting Old Delhi, fascinated by its sights, smells and sounds. Phupijan, my father's younger sister, lived in Haveli Hisamuddin Haider, Ballimaran. Inhabited mainly by the Punjabi Saudagaran. Part of this mohalla is known as Punjabi Phatak. Mamoo Ilyas, my mother's elder brother, lived in the neighbouring mohalla, Ahata Kaley Sahab. We called on them often and they fed me with delights not available elsewhere.

The habshi halwa sohan from Hanif, whose shop is at the entrance of the Punjabi Phatak, is still my family's favourite mithai. As a young boy, Hanif had worked as a domestic help with the Chatriwaley, a Saudagaran family. When he became older, they helped him establish a milk supply business. Later, they taught him how to make the

Natraj Dahi Bhalla Corner

Aloo tikki at Natraj

Dahi bhalla at Natraj

Jalebi from Old Famous Jalebi Wala

habshi halwa sohan with their family recipe and assisted him in setting up this small shop. Prepared with milk, sugar and desi ghee, the halwa is available from October to March. The summer heat melts the ghee that binds the habshi halwa.

I remember relishing daulat ki chaat, made in winter from doodh ka jhaag, milk froth, that was served on leaves. I enjoyed malai ki baraf, layers of frozen cream that vendors carried it in quaint looking wooden boxes surrounded by ice.

Family favourites are the sunheri gajar halwa, prepared with golden coloured carrots and gheeghwar halwa made with aloe vera from Sheeren Bhavan in Chitli Qabar. Both are winter specialities made with desi ghee. Among other popular and delicious mithai and savouries are Chaina Ram's *sev ki mithai* called sevpaak, and karachi halwa. Sending mithai on festive occasions from Chaina Ram was considered a sign of prosperity. Desi ghee kachori and daalbiji from Kanwarji are another addiction. It's an old street side

The famous jalebi wala at Chandni Chowk

shop on Chandni Chowk at the entrance of Paranthe Wali Gali. I am not a fan of the parantha from this iconic gali as they are deep fried. Besides, these eateries are not as old as they claim.

A visit to the old city is never complete without the thick round desi ghee jalebi from the Old Famous Jalebiwala, whose shop is in Chandni Chowk at the corner of Dariba Kalan. A plate of dahi badey from Natraj, the small corner kiosk is another must. The shop is adjacent to the Central Bank, so these were called '*Central Bank key dahi badey*'. On hearing about these as a child, I often wondered why the bank was selling dahi badey. Shiv Mishtan Bhandar is another shop at the entrance of Kucha Ghasi Ram that has been known for bedmi aloo poori, kachori and other savouries made with desi ghee.

In our part of the world, it is said that Muslims are not good at making mithai and *namkeen*, savouries. My relatives who migrated to Pakistan crave for these and it's the best gift one can send them.

After dinner, my cousins would bring home milk from the large

Savouries from Kunwarji's

A well-known food stall at Chandni Chowk
Photo: Vaseem Ahmed Dehlvi

kadhai. Piping hot and served with heaps of pistachio and almond garnish in *abkhora*, clay bowls; the fragrance of the earth fused with milk is extraordinary. The clay absorbs the excess moisture of the milk and it turns thick. Stalls selling this milk are in Matia Mahal, which is close to Jama Masjid. Having a cup of hot kadhai milk after dinner continues to be a popular tradition with Dilliwalas.

Favoured breakfasts in the old city consist of aloo poori, sliced potatoes with herbs and deep-fried poori. Small eateries in Ballimaran and Maliwara are famous for them. Chaina Ram serves delicious aloo poori from eight to eleven in the morning.

Chaina Ram has been in Chandni Chowk since 1901

Sevpak mithai from Chaina Ram

Bedmi aloo poori from Shiv Mishthan Bhandar
Photo: Vaseem Ahmed Dehlvi

Baqerkhani roti being prepared in the old city

Dilli Dastarkhwan

Favoured meat on the Dilli dastarkhwan are goat mutton, chicken and fish. *Titar*, partridge, and *batair*, quail, once popular delicacies are no longer part of the regular spread. Except for nihari and kebab, beef is not appreciated. Apart from being viewed as a poor man's meat, beef is considered taxing on the digestive system. When making qeema, mincemeat, I buy the mutton on the bone and then have it minced. I usually use the bones for soup stock. My mother always objects and insists that the bones be cooked with the mincemeat so that it looks like goat mutton and not beef. Beef bones are much larger and easily identified by their size.

Beef is traditionally referred to as *badey ka gosht* and mutton, as *chotey ka gosht*. These are terms unique to Muslim terminology in the subcontinent. While travelling on the road in the interiors of Uttar Pradesh, a friend recalled seeing a signboard in Urdu on a roadside kebab shop that read, '*Khuda ki qasam, chotey ke hain!*' Implying, I swear by God, the kebab are made from mutton!

Traditionally, men of the house purchase raw meat from the *qasai*, butcher. Among my female cousins, I am probably one of the few who goes to butcher shops. Once upon a time in the mohallas, men left to buy *gosht tarkaari*, meat and vegetable, after the *fajr namaz*, the mandatory prayer just before sunrise. Men of our community still do the grocery shopping and most venture out in the morning. Even now, vegetable vendors in mohallas begin selling at dawn. Ever since the government's order to move abattoirs to the city outskirts, fresh mutton has been arriving late in the markets.

Dilliwalas remain extremely particular about meat cuts, preferring portions of *adla,* shank, *dast,* shoulder, *put,* back, *gardan,* neck, *seena,* breast, and *raan,* leg. We tease others for usually buying meat without knowing and specifying the cuts. Punjabis tend to prefer *chaap,* chops. We don't use chops in our curries, they are barbecued, grilled or panfried. Whenever I go to the butcher, he tells me to wait saying, '*Aap ke liye to araam se banyenge*,' we will take time to prepare meat for you. He knows how finicky we are and that poor-quality meat or bad cuts will not be tolerated.

We always use goat mutton and never lamb, which is tough and has a *heek*, distinct smell. In fact, if someone serves tough pieces of meat, negative comments follow such as, '*Allah maaf karey, bhed ka gosht lag raha tha*,' May God forgive, it seems they served lamb. Considering how Dilliwalas scorn lamb, I am amused when reputed restaurants serve it with aplomb.

We grew up learning that different parts of the goat have separate properties. Eating the neck portion gets rid of fever and *paya*, trotters, helps strengthen bones, particularly beneficial in healing fractures. The broth of *choosa*, tender chicken, will help regain vitality after illnesses. Mamoo Abdullah told me that *kapoora* and *gurda*, testicle and kidney, have aphrodisiacal properties. He said that in bygone days, these were fed to the bridegroom and his close friends at wedding parties. These meat portions are not added to regular mutton dishes.

On special occasions nargisi koftey, biryani, qorma, shaami kebab and other elaborate dishes are made. Murgh musallam, whole chicken stuffed with boiled eggs and dry fruits, was once a banquet favourite. Festivities are never complete without baqerkhani and qulcha, special varieties of Delhi roti.

It is said that the baqerkhani roti was created and patented by Mr Baqer Khan during the days of Bahadur Shah Zafar. Bread makers needed a licence from the Royal Fort to duplicate the roti. Lighter and fluffier than the baqerkhani, the qulcha roti has become equally popular. Both these breads are made with wheat kneaded in milk, ghee and sugar. Qulcha uses egg as an additional ingredient and ferments easily. The baqerkhani is flatter and the use of excessive ghee makes it slightly heavier to digest. Unlike the

A biryani degh

qulcha, baqerkhani can be stored for days. Nowadays, people tend to confuse baqerkhani with sheermal, which is from the Avadh cuisine. The two are quite different in colour, texture and taste.

The layered warqi parantha, ghee ki roti and chapati are other varieties of breads made for daily consumption. What we call chapati is popularly called rumali roti. This is probably because it is as thin as a rumal, handkerchief. Frankly, Dilliwalas find this terminology obscene as what we call rumali is the small diamond-shaped piece of cloth stitched in the crotch area of men and women's pajamas. Attached to the seams of the right and left leg of the pajama, the rumali allows free movement without causing the seams to tear. It remains a unique feature of Muslim tailoring in the subcontinent.

Chapati or rumali roti is made on what others commonly call *ulta tava*, a round inverted cooking utensil for roti, which for us is *seedha* tava. In most Dilliwala homes, a rotiwali goes from house-

Qalai process of tin plating on copper degh

to-house to makes the day's roti for them. These are so well made
that the roti doesn't turn hard and can be lightly reheated. Since
it is a specialized skill, many of us, including me, have switched to
eating phulka. It puffs up on a flat tava. Our phulka is much larger
though, almost double the size of the phulka made in most homes.

Dilliwalas are exceedingly particular about *taseer*, effect of food
on the body. I grew up relating to food in terms of *halka*, light,
bhaari, heavy, *garam*, warm, or *thanda*, cold. Spices such as cardamoms,
cloves, cinnamon, and peppercorns are believed to have garam taseer,
warming effect. Dishes which have these as ingredients are cooked

mostly in winter. Young unmarried girls were often prohibited from having egg yolk or large quantities of heavily spiced food lest the garam taseer send their hormones into sexual overdrive! These rules are not just for young girls. Ammi still advises me to keep my twenty-four-year-old unmarried son on a largely vegetarian diet for the same reason. In hushed whispers Mamoo Abdullah told me that is was said that Muslim courtesans had an edge in their profession because of their and spicy non-vegetarian diet!

Food is traditionally cooked in copper utensils with tin plating. In the old city, getting *qalai*, tin plating, done is relatively easy as qalaiwalas often roam from door-to-door offering their services. We never use stainless steel utensils to cook, and many in the family continue cooking in copper pots and pans. It is said that cooking in copper utensils enhances the taste and adds minerals to the food.

Interestingly, one can usually identify a Muslim-owned street side eatery by the kind of cooking utensils on the stove. They cook in copper deghs while others invariably cook in stainless steel or brass pots and pans.

Ammi tells me how food was once served in a *rakabi*, small round copper plate with tin plating. These had decorative frill like edgings and the depth of porridge bowls. The depth helps in holding *shorba*, gravy. Usually, two or three people ate from one rakabi. Earlier, mithai distributed at weddings and births would be sent in a rakabi or a copper *katora*, bowl, with calligraphic engravings marking the occasion.

The use of pressure cookers or easily available aluminium alloy *pateeliyan*, cooking pots, is now common. Earlier *matti ki handiyan*, clay pots, were used for dal and *ghotwa saag*, crushed spinach. Some clay pots had polished interiors so that oil-based dishes could be prepared in them. Cooking in clay adds a delicate earthy flavour.

Martbaan, large jars of ceramic, were used to store pickles. When girls got married, they were given varieties of ceramic and copper

Professional cooks in the old city

utensils for their new home. These included *seeni*, large round trays, cooking pots of various sizes, and a *salafchi*, specially styled jug and bowl that were brought to the *dastarkhwan*, table spread. Someone would take the salafchi around for people to wash their hands before and after meals.

In the old days, the medium used for cooking was desi ghee, clarified butter. I remember dozens of desi ghee containers made of tin stacked in the kitchen pantry. These were purchased from villagers who came to sell ghee to their customers in the city. Those who could not afford desi ghee mostly cooked in the Dalda brand of vegetable ghee. Mamoo Abdullah said many families would hide their Dalda cans as their presence suggested that they were not a *khata peeta gharana,* prosperous home.

Sometime during the mid-eighties, desi ghee began to be replaced by vegetable oils. Desi ghee, expensive as it has become, is largely reserved for *bhagar*, topping, parantha and home-made sweet dishes.

Despite her rising levels of cholesterol, Ammi cannot do without desi ghee and credits her good health to it. She loves to quote the old proverb, '*Ghee banaye salan, badi bahu ka naam,*' suggesting that even though the daughter-in-law gets the credit for the cooking, it is the ghee that makes food delicious.

Ammi keeps experimenting with various brands of desi ghee available in the market. Each time I enter her kitchen, I see a new brand. Ammi's friends from smaller towns know unadulterated desi ghee is the best gift for her. Now, with doctors saying that a little desi ghee is good for health, quarrels with Ammi over her obsession have ceased.

We often say that you either have *haath main lazzat* or you don't! This suggests that while some just rustle up anything and it turns out to be delicious, others may work hard at cooking but just don't seem to get it right! Ammi believes that this has to do with the condition of one's heart. She says that God grants *lazzat*, taste, and *barakat*, blessing, to the food cooked with love and *acchi niyat*, good intent.

My aunts and cousins at our home for a family gathering, 1974

My cousin Farah's birthday party at home, 1970

A Community Life

Living with an extended family resulted in some festivity or the other taking place at home around the year. Mothers were not allowed to breastfeed new-borns before the *phupi,* father's sister, was rewarded with *doodh dhulai,* suckling gift money. The aunt then proceeded to wash the mother's breasts and held the baby to them. In those days, childbirth took place at home with the help of midwives, which is why these customs were possible. In modern hospitals, the aunts would probably be thrown out for handling newborn babies with utter disregard for infections.

However, two Islamic traditions continue to this day. Almost immediately after birth, a family elder whispers the azaan, call to prayer, in the infant's ear. This is to remind the child of his or her primordial covenant with the Divine. The second tradition is that a drop of honey is fed to the infant almost immediately after birth.

Usually, on the seventh day after the child's birth, there is an *aqeeqah,* a ceremony where the newborn's hair is removed. The occasion is marked by *qurbani,* sacrifice, of a goat. This is done as soon as the barber shaves off the hair. Most people remain particular about this coordination. In some cases, where the child's hair is removed on western shores or in a place not conducive to animal sacrifice, a phone call is made to inform the butcher to instantly place the knife on the goat's jugular. Some of this meat is distributed to the poor, some amongst friends and relatives and the rest kept by the family for a feast.

Another family celebration is held after the *khatna,* circumcision, of male children. This is usually done when the boy is a week old. When babies first eat solids at three or four months, they are fed a light rice pudding at a *kheer chatai* ceremony.

When a child is four years old, a Bismillah ceremony takes place that celebrates a child's first lesson in reading the Quran.

The function involves a family elder or an Imam helping the child recite a few words from the Quran. After the feasting, gift-wrapped mithai, usually balushahi, is distributed amongst the guests.

Each occasion requires a different preparation. It is a tradition that before making anything else in the kitchen, a newly-wed bride first cook kheer, or any other sweet dish. Earlier, the groom's family tested her cooking skills by keeping both salt and white ground sugar in front of her. In jest, they waited for the shy bride to recognize the difference and choose the right ingredient.

Expectant and nursing mothers are fed nourishing sweets like panjiri and satora made from dry fruits, desi ghee and semolina. In yesteryears, the bride's family sent similar preparations for the groom, prior to the wedding, to prepare him for conjugal duties.

On joyous occasions, a *hissa*, share, of the mithai, is sent to relatives and friends. The duty of distributing food, fruits and mithai was traditionally given to the *kahar*, who could be compared to modern day courier service. In those days, kahars went door-to-door in the mohalla delivering food. Two kahars carry a degh on their shoulders with the help of two wooden rods.

Despite most families from the Saudagaran community having moved from the mohallas, sending wedding invitations through courier is still not the norm. Cards are personally delivered by siblings, aunts, uncles and cousins of the bride and groom who come together to share this responsibility. Wedding venues still have segregated areas for men and women. One of the first few women in our biradari to discontinue wearing the burqa, my mother did not follow these old customs.

Long intervals between engagements and weddings, which were once the norm are not preferred any more. Families would regularly exchange gifts to strengthen the bond. Seasonal fruits sent to the betrothed's house were known as *samaal*. Ostensibly sent for *dulhan ke chakhne ke liye*, a sampling for the bride, the samaal came not in kilos but in multiples of tons: mangoes, melons and watermelons, pomegranate, apples, litchis and other fruits. The samaal filled the entire *aangan*, courtyard, of the old havelis. This would be distributed amongst neighbours, friends and extended family. These gifts had to be of good quality as the living standard of a family was judged on their basis. I remember the elders mentioning an engagement that was called off because the would-be in-laws sent a samaal of water chestnuts. The family compared the chestnuts to the thorns of hell and felt insulted at this display of mediocrity.

Sometimes fruits such as mangoes, pineapples and apples would be taken to a *barafkhana*, ice factory, and frozen in blocks of ice before being sent to family and friends. This not only appeared beautiful, but helped to keep the fruit from rotting since refrigerators were not common then. Distribution on such a large scale is almost impossible these days. This activity is now more or less restricted to immediate neighbours and family.

If Eid al Azha, Feast of Sacrifice, falls during the period of engagement, it remains customary for the boy's family to send the *qurbani ka bakra*, the sacrificial goat, for the girl. Ammi recalls that the goat sent for her was purchased for a thousand rupees. This was during the mid-fifties, when an average goat would cost five or six rupees. The animal came decorated with white metal jewellery, dressed in brocade cloth with gold and silver embroidery. The obese goat could barely stand and came with instructions that it should be seated on a chaarpai and fed just jalebi made with desi ghee.

In the past, wedding banquets included qorma, biryani, baqerkhani and kheer or zarda. In fact, till some decades ago, this was all that the wedding menu consisted of. These days wedding have become lavish with far too many varieties of food.

Shama Kothi

A 1954 edition of *Shama* magazine

Shama Kothi

My grandfather, Hafiz Yusuf Dehlvi, whom we called Abba, lived in Phatak Habash Khan. Once a gated mohalla, it extends from Novelty Cinema to Khari Baoli, the spice market. It is named after Sidi Miftah, a slave from Habash, Abyssinia, who rose to great heights during Emperor Shah Jahan's rule. He became known as Habash Khan and was gifted vast landholdings. My mother's family lived in Baada Hindu Rao before moving to Ballimaran during the Partition.

Zeenat Kauser, my mother, was then eleven years old. At sixteen she married Yunus Dehlvi, my father, who had just completed his masters in philosophy from St Stephen's College. It was a grand wedding with the street lanes from Ballimaran to Phatak Habash Khan decorated with festive lights. The number of guests was exceptionally large, with over a hundred relatives and friends from outside Delhi. Dozens of cooks were hired to cater meals for the guests.

In 1938, Abba founded and edited *Shama*, an Urdu film and literary magazine that became very popular. In 1943, at the age of thirteen and still in school, Daddy founded and edited *Khilona*, a children's magazine in Urdu. He created its iconic characters, Mian Fauladi, Iron man, and Nastoor, a mischievous young jinn, who studied at Maulvi Sahab's school and enthralled the children with his magical powers. A whole generation of children from Urdu-speaking families learnt Urdu language with *Khilona*. Later, many eminent people including the erstwhile president Dr Zakir Hussain were amongst the magazine's contributors. My father made the *Shama* monthly Adabi Muamma, a literary crossword, that acquired an iconic status. It gave prizes worth lakhs of rupees and sometimes, in kilos of gold.

The house we grew up in was named after *Shama*. A.P. Kanvinde, a leading architect of those times, designed Shama Kothi. The address was 11 Sardar Patel Marg. One entrance of the kothi fell at the corner

L-R: My father at his wedding with his younger brothers Ilyas and Idrees Dehlvi

Daddy, Ammi, Faheem and I

of Sardar Patel Marg while the other gate was on Kautilya Marg. The two-storeyed residence, spread over almost 2,500 square yards, had sprawling gardens, ponds with lilies, dozens of rooms, verandahs, balconies and water fountains. Having lived in a congested mohalla, Abba wanted the new house to have large open spaces.

The locals referred to our home as *paani waali kothi*, the house with water, because there were provisions for refrigerated drinking water for passers by. A huge Voltas water cooler stood in one corner inside the garden and its taps were located on the outside wall along Sardar Patel Marg. Abba installed this facility *Fi Sabilillah*, for the sake of Allah. Through the decades that we lived there, cyclists, motorists, pedestrians, taxis and buses carrying passengers would stop to quench their thirst. In those days, bottled and packaged drinking water was not easily available. When the cooling machine malfunctioned, dozens of complaints were passed on to us through the chowkidars till the problem was fixed.

Vimla Sindhi, who worked at the house of then Prime Minister Jawahar Lal Nehru, often visited our home. Nehru's residence at Teen Murti was close to Shama Kothi. Vimlaji told Daddy that once, while passing by our house, Nehru noticed the crowd outside and enquired about it. He was informed that they were there to drink water. Nehru asked if there were any such arrangements for the crowds that poured into his home. On hearing the negative response, Nehru instructed that similar facilities be installed immediately.

After our ancestral house was sold in 2002, I moved to a flat in Nizamuddin East. In continuation of Abba's tradition, I tie a large *matka*, clay pot, containing drinking water to a tree opposite my home. These days matkas fitted with taps are easily available. It gladdens my heart to see local hawkers, drivers, maids and others who pass by quench their thirst. Another of Abba's habits that I try to emulate is to not eat before feeding the birds. Abba would scatter some bajra in the lawn for the birds every day before sitting down to his lunch.

I had heard from family elders that our house was often referred to as 'Dilli ka Taj Mahal'. I thought it was an exaggeration, till some older friends from the city, including Satish Gujral, artist and architect, confirmed this story. He told me that in the sixties, architecture students were taken to look at the grand white exterior of Shama Kothi.

Because of its corner location and impressive facade, Shama Kothi appeared larger than its actual size. Often, it would be mistaken for a hotel. Tourist buses and taxis regularly enquired about reservations. Most of them were headed for Hotel Diplomat, which was two buildings away at number nine. The hotel did not have an imposing hotel-like structure and could easily be missed. Sometimes, foreigners turned up in our home in the middle of the night asking for their rooms.

The driveway of Shama Kothi led to a large porch with the main entrance door of the home. Through all the years we lived there, this door remained open. With so many open corridors around the house, it was impossible to lock it. So strangers sometimes knocked on our bedroom doors.

This mix up with Hotel Diplomat created a comedy of errors. One summer night, Apa Saeeda, our family retainer, was sleeping in the verandah on her chaarpai. Expecting her cousin who lived in Calcutta to come visiting, Ammi had instructed Apa Saeeda that the guest room be provided for him. Ammi's cousin was very fair, looked and dressed like a 'Yurpean' as Nani, my maternal grandmother, would say. Resembling a European was the ultimate compliment she gave someone!

In the darkness of the night, Apa Saeeda was woken up by a fair skin visitor asking for his room. Mistaking him for Ammi's cousin, she led him to the guest room. When she switched on the light, Apa Saeeda came face to face with the stranger. Scared, she screamed and came running into my bedroom. We sorted out the confusion

Amma and Abba with their family

and I directed him to Hotel Diplomat. A livid Apa Saeeda took the
sleeping watchman to task.

Abba did not interfere with the architect's design except when it
came to the cooking area. He believed that an outsider could never
understand the kitchen requirements of us Dilliwalas. Kanvinde had
no say in the kitchen and thus, it remained the shabbiest part of the
house. The walls made of *pindole,* a yellowish substance made from
kuchi mitti, unbaked earth, looked patchy against the swanky marble
flooring in the rest of the house. I recall the *bawarchikhana* forever filled
with smoke. Badruddin, the old bearded family khansaama, cook, blew
with all his might at the *chiptiyan,* wooden shavings, over coal fuel with
a *phukni,* heavy iron pipe, to raise the flames on the earthen stoves.

The pantry adjoined the kitchen. Here, sugar, grains, rice, wheat,
pulses and masalas were stored in large brown *boriyan,* jute sacks.
Kitchen stocks were purchased in quantities of *mann,* not kilograms.
One mann equals approximately forty kilograms. Wheat, lentils and
rice were bought with the change of seasons. Ammi modernized
the kitchen in the eighties, long after Badruddin died.

My Apa Saeeda

Apa Saeeda – A Childhood Bond

Apa Saeeda was a sort of surrogate mother to my brothers and me, continually assuring, '*Main tumhaare paas hoon na*,' I am with you. She bathed, clothed and fed us with motherly affection. She slept with us in our room. In the middle of the night, I often crawled out of bed and snuggled up to her. Her smell and touch comforted me like nothing else in the world. We loved her so much that at times the strong bond we shared made Ammi envious!

Apa Saeeda came from Baghpat and had been married in her early teens. Soon after the marriage, she learnt that her husband had remarried. Her dignity injured, Apa Saeeda walked out of the marriage. Ammi told me this story when I had grown up. Apa Saeeda herself never spoke about her hurtful past.

Apa Saeeda entered our lives through her mother, who often visited Nana, my maternal grandfather's house. She was friends with my grandmother and occasionally helped with housework. Ammi prevailed upon Apa Saeeda's mother to allow her to live with us. Faheem, my elder brother, was then around five years of age, I was three and Vaseem, my younger brother, was a few months old. I have no recollection of life without Apa Saeeda's soft, compassionate and reassuring face. With no children of her own, her world came to revolve around us three siblings. Images of her in a beige or white knee-length kurta, churidaar pyjama and crisp cotton dupatta remain alive in my heart.

During the British period, some exclusive clubs, hotels and restaurants came up in the city. During the sixties and seventies, Ammi and Daddy went out almost every evening for high tea to Gaylord in Regal building at Connaught Place. We were never taken along to this 'adult activity'. With a hectic social life, my parents were rarely home.

Apa Saeeda kept us from complaining about their absence,

coming up with ingenious ways to entertain us. When Ammi and
Daddy went to the movies, we were left at home. Apa Saeeda
promised us our own movies. As we lay on our beds, she handwove
stories around the shadows of the traffic on the main road that
fell on the bedroom wall. Since there was not much traffic then,
we occasionally spotted the shadow of a bullock cart or a lorry.
Apa Saeeda cleverly used her fingers to create animal shadows that
became magnified with the reflected light falling on the wall. The
Central Ridge Reserve Forest fell just across our home. We heard
the nocturnal cries of hyenas and jackals. Apa Saeeda weaved these
into the tales. An enchanting storyteller, her stories revolved around
rajas, ranis, magicians and dacoits in villages. In the morning, we
woke up to find popcorn packets and chocolates under our pillows,
quietly placed there by our guilty parents.

We went for walks around Diplomatic Enclave and frequently
sat on the grass under the shade of the treess. In springtime, we
collected kachnar flowers strewn on the pavements. Apa Saeeda tied
these loosely to one end of her dupatta and brought them home. She
cooked delicious dishes with these flowers.

It was Apa Saeeda who initiated me into the art of cooking. She
believed that girls must learn *ghardaari*, housekeeping skills. When I
argued that Ammi never knew how to cook, she replied, 'Your Ammi
is a *shahzadi*, princess. May Allah always keep her in this grandiose
style. There are a dozen of us to look after her needs. May Allah bless
you with a similar destiny, but life cannot be trusted. Only Allah
knows what your destiny is. If you go to your marital home and
don't know how to cook, they will blame me for bringing you up
badly. And you know that I can put up with anything but *beizzati,*
disrespect. Do you want people to point fingers at me?' That sealed
it for me. I loved Apa Saeeda with all my heart and soul. The mere
thought that someone might dare defame her seemed sinful. So,
when Apa Saeeda cooked, I watched and learned.

She ensured that we ate our meals on time and without fussing about the contents of the spread. If we did not listen, she employed a standard trick. She would call out to one of the staff boys, 'Rasheed, *la mera burqa*,' get my burqa. This meant that Apa Saeeda was preparing to leave. She wore a white cotton tent-like burqa when going by bus for her occasional visit to Baghpat. Her sister's family lived there. The threat always worked and we obeyed immediately since none of us wanted her to leave.

The same threat seemed to work with my parents. Apa Saeeda could not bear anyone, including Ammi, scolding us siblings. If Ammi became harsh with us, Apa Saeeda said, '*Saaf baat hai, ham apne bachon ke saath ziyaadti nahin dekh saktey*,' making it clear that she would not put up with her children being rebuked. She protected us from punishments and we got away with quite a lot of mischief.

Apa Saeeda took Ammi doing any chore as a great offence and insult to her person. If she found Ammi fiddling in the kitchen to even make a cup of tea, she would get upset saying, '*Kya mai mar gayi?*' Am I dead? Ammi rarely got in Apa Saeeda's way or dared comment that we were being overfed. She did once, and Apa Saeeda accused her of casting *nazar*, evil eye, on 'her' children and told her not to interfere in what 'her' kids ate.

Baghpat remained a threatening word throughout my childhood. It symbolized something that took Apa Saeeda away from us. She had a niece called Waseema who lived in Baghpat. Apa Saeeda loved her and that made me feel jealous. I remember telling her that I wished Waseema would die so we could have her all to ourselves!

On reaching the age of five, both my brothers and I were admitted to boarding schools in Shimla. Later, some of our cousins joined us in the school. Ammi was very no-nonsense mother and believed that Apa Saeeda's and my grandmother's mollycoddling and indulgence was spoiling us kids. My parents thought we needed discipline and sent us away from home.

A family photo clicked at Mahatta & Co., Delhi, 1965

A birthday party at home

The girls of Shama Kothi were sent to Loreto Convent Tara Hall and the boys to Bishop Cotton School. The longest spells we came home for were the three-month long winter holidays. Convinced that the schools did not provide us enough nourishing food, Apa Saeeda pampered us with all kinds of food and fruit throughout the holidays. She tried hard to hide the tears that began flowing long before the holidays ended. Occasionally, she visited us in Shimla during our short school breaks.

Apa Saeeda lived with us till around twenty years ago. Old and weak, she then moved to her family home in Baghpat. I feel blessed that she lived to hold my son in her arms. We pleaded with her to continue staying with us and wanted to look after her. She adamantly refused, saying she did not want to become a burden. Sometimes she came to visit us for a few days and at times we went to meet her.

Some years ago, when I last met Apa Saeeda at Baghpat, she had been affected by Alzheimer's disease. Despite her failing memory, she recognized me. I wrapped myself around her, laying my head in her lap as always. She blessed me and wanted to know if I had eaten. Clinging on to her, I wept and she wiped the tears. A few weeks later, we heard that she had left us forever. I went to Baghpat to grieve together with Apa Naeema, her sister, and Waseema. They showed me a little bundle consisting of all of Apa Saeeda's belongings: a few clothes, her unused passport and some pictures of my brothers and me.

Not a single day passes without memories of my wise and beautiful Apa Saeeda. The values she taught help me wade through life. Her cooking tips echo in my head as I stir the pot. Whenever I cook langar, food for distribution, I offer prayers for Apa Saeeda that her soul rest in peace. Inshallah, God willing, we shall meet on the other side.

Abba, my brother and I in his lap

Growing up with Amma and Abba

My father had two younger brothers, Idrees Dehlvi and Ilyas Dehlvi, whom we called Badey uncle and Chotey uncle. Along with Abba and Daddy, they were a part of *Shama* and other Shama Group publications.

The delightful aspect of growing up in a joint family was that there were many children. Badey uncle had two boys, Sajid and Kaleem, and Fridaus, a girl. Chotey uncle had three girls, Farah, Rasia and Sarah, and Mohsin, a boy. I was the eldest of the girls and my brother, the eldest of the boys. Both my uncles had women retainers for their families who were called Bua. One was referred to as Farah's Bua, and the other as Fridaus's Bua.

Often, other cousins would come and spend days on end at Shama Kothi. Sometimes they went to school from our home. When close relatives left on a pilgrimage to Mecca or a holiday, they left their kids with Amma, my grandmother. Any given time, there were nearly a dozen or more kids prancing around.

Our evenings were spent in the garden playing games like *pithoo, aankhmicholi, langdi taang, chor sipahi* and cricket. We could play in the garden till about fifteen minutes before sunset. We had to move indoors and could resume playing outdoors after the sun set completely. This time of dusk is referred to as *dono waqt mil rahe hain*, the meeting of two time frames. Amma and Apa Saeeda said it was the time when the jinns stepped out. Since jinns are known to harass young girls and boys, it was best to stay clear of them.

Playtime was interrupted in the early evening for *doodh ka waqt,* milk break. Apa Saeeda and the two Bua brought glasses of milk, which had to be drunk before we could resume play. Tea for children remained out of the question. When Apa Saeeda drank tea and I wished to sip some, she frowned and retorted, '*Chai se dimaagh mey khushki ho jayegi, doodh piyo*,' tea dehydrates the brain, drink milk.

Childhood habits die hard and all of us continue to be obsessed with a daily milk fix.

When we kids fought amongst ourselves, the three women took sides, with each defending their brood and accusing the other kids of bad behaviour. But like us, they quickly resumed their friendship, becoming a watchful trio again. A favourite outdoor activity was cycling. We rented cycles from the local market at two rupees an hour. With the roads not being crowded, we were permitted to cycle in the neighbourhood. On returning, Apa Saeeda readied our snack of French toast. I doubt if those were French in origin, but that's what we called the slices of fried toast that were dipped in batter made from egg, milk and sugar. It made for a healthy and wholesome snack. Thick potato fries with tomato ketchup was another favourite. So were Britannia bread slices topped with condensed milk or layers of fresh malai, cream, and honey.

After the sunset, when the jinns had passed, Amma packed us off in our Comet and Dodge convertible cars to India Gate for ice cream. A company called 'Joy Ice Creams' first introduced mango duet ice cream bars. It became a reputed brand but disappeared after some years. In a promotional scheme, the company once offered a pack of playing cards on the purchase of two mango duet bars. We bought them by the dozen and ended up with stacks of cards. That's when we learnt to play cards, but secretly, as the elders disapproved. We mostly played something called *teen do paanch,* three, two and five. Once Abba spotted us playing a card game and made us throw away all the packs in the garbage can. He said playing cards could lead to the bad habit of gambling, something *haram,* not permissible in our religion.

One of the few restaurants that my parents took us to was an open-air place called Rambles. This wonderful restaurant stood where the Palika Bazaar parking is today. In the seventies, Rambles was a very popular hangout. We loved going there especially on summer evenings. I relished their cold coffee with ice cream, while my younger brother went straight for the Banana Split. An *Archies* comic junkie, he loved Jughead's favourite ice cream. This, along with chicken sandwiches, was part of our staple order at Rambles.

The large number of children frolicking around in Shama Kothi sometimes misled outsiders into thinking that a play school existed on the premises. I remember a stranger walking into the garden and asking Amma about it. After replying in the negative, Amma told us to go and play in the smaller garden that was covered with a larger hedge. This made us less visible from the main road. Amma whispered, '*Nazar lag jayegi*,' scared of the evil eye being cast on her large brood.

Warding off nazar is typically done with food items. Apa Saeeda would make us lie down and would then take seven whole red chillies with unbroken stems. She circled them around us seven times, ensuring the chillies touched our bodies. Then she burnt them at the stove. If there were no *dhaans*, fumes to choke the breath, Apa Saeeda would tell Amma, '*Nazar jal gayi*,' the evil has been warded off.

My mother preferred removing the evil eye with eggs. She made us stand while circling our bodies three times with one whole raw egg. She would then ask us to throw it over the left shoulder in a garbage bin and ensure that the egg broke. If afflicted with a sickness that needed an immediate antidote, three eggs were used one after the other. Ammi still practices this method. Now that we live in flats, the eggs are flushed down the toilet. I hate to confess this, but I do the same thing to Arman Ali, my son who is now twenty-four years old!

To keep the house protected from *bala*, tribulations, every *mangal*, Tuesday, and *hafta*, Saturday mornings, Amma had *cheechdey*, inedible meat scraps, littered on the terrace for *cheel kavey*, kites and crows. These scraps of meat were purchased separately from the butcher. Ammi also did this through the many decades we lived at Shama

Me as a child   My brother Faheem and I

Kothi. After having shifted to a flat without terrace rights, such indulgences are no longer possible. Ammi remains content to feed the birds bajra and the crows with breadcrumbs on her balcony. In mohallas of the old city, vendors still go around selling scraps of meat, mostly *phepdey*, goat lungs, for people to feed the crows.

Most families in our community provide food for at least one or two people every day. Often it is sent to a local mosque for the Imam and his students or companions. This is charity given from whatever is cooked for the family. Food is shared with the belief that God will grant '*Risq main barakat*,' an increase in provisions.

Abba had a generous and compassionate heart. The kitchen areas of Shama Kothi seemed to forever have large cauldrons of food specially made for distribution. Friends who visited our home recall how they rarely left without being served a meal. After a party, Ammi would often pack some briyani, qorma and baqerkhani roti for my friends to take home. Some of them say that they never saw a house with so much food around all the time.

Abba remained particular about the large number of domestic staff eating the same food as the family. I remember a distant aunt expressing shock at the way our staff helped themselves to whatever they wanted from the kitchen. She chided my mother for being a careless housekeeper, advising her to keep food provisions locked and give measured hand-outs for staff consumption. Ammi replied that those who locked food had locks on their hearts. She added that the food did not belong to her, '*Daane daane par likha hota hai khaney waley ka naam*,' each grain of food has the name of the person for whom it is destined.

At Shama Kothi, there were two sessions for dinner. The children were given an early dinner while the adults ate later. Similar to our boarding school routine, dinner was announced using a hammer on a gong bell. This was kept on a shelf in the dining room, which had a twenty-four-seat table in the centre.

Lunch and dinner usually consisted of three or four main dishes that were mostly mutton based. Seasonal vegetables like peas, beetroot, spinach, turnips, carrots and cauliflower were added to meat. In summer, dal and rice were frequently served.

While masoor, moong and other dal were served, rajma was never cooked at home. I grew up associating rajma with my Hindu friends! I relished it in their homes and became rather fascinated with its taste. Vegetables such as brinjal, cabbage and pumpkin had no place in our kitchens either. Sometimes fruit including bananas, pears and apples were cooked with mutton.

My childhood memories are of Amma constantly hovering around the kitchen and pantry. Along with her retinue of women retainers, she sat in the veranda, surrounded by food items. Seeni were filled with spices. These were were kept in the sun for drying. Amma busied herself supervising the grinding of spices and making seasonal pickles. Apa Saeeda helped Amma with preserving the pickles in earthenware jars, leaving them exposed to the sun to mature.

All essential masalas including turmeric powder, coriander powder and red chilli powder were prepared at home. These were ground in an *imam dasta*, mortar and pestle. Some spices were ground on the *sil*, stone slab, with a *silbatta*, stone crusher. Long after Amma left us, ground masala from reliable shops in Khari Baoli began to be used.

Amma maintained a vegetable patch behind the bedrooms, adjoining the rear side of the boundary wall. Although the produce did not fulfil all our requirements, Amma delighted in cooking home-grown vegetables. After her death, my mother planted trees in that area for no one seemed interested in growing vegetables.

Despite having a large-sized fridge, Amma kept her stock of ginger underground. She had a foot-long pit dug in one corner of the garden, where she buried the ginger. She pulled out some as and when required. This method ensured that the ginger remained fresh. I doubt if anyone follows these old ways anymore.

Abba and Amma did not approve of us coming late to the table after the food had been served. Abba would say, '*Khaney ko interzar nahin karvatey,*' don't make food wait for you. He said it was against the teachings of Islam. He seemed upset whenever Daddy would excuse himself from joining the family for meals on account of work. Abba would say, '*Insaan khaney ke liye hi to kamata hai,*' after all we earn to fill our bellies.

Abba ruled that the family had to eat at least one meal in a day together. Since his dinner consisted solely of a cup of milk, we all came together for lunch. Daddy and my uncles were away at office during weekdays, so the women and children joined Abba, who came home for lunch. He maintained that families who eat together, stay together. Although the three families continued to stay together after Abba's death, they gradually began cooking and eating separately. The strong bond between them was never quite the same again.

Amma set the rules for the daily food routine. Despite the presence of a skilled cook and other kitchen staff, her *bahus*, daughters-in-law,

Family elders, my cousins and I

had to set the menu and supervise the cooking. Two days of the week this responsibility fell on each of the three daughters-in-law. On Sundays, Amma supervised these duties. Shamim Auntie and Ameena Auntie were terrific at cooking. My mother did not enjoy kitchen chores. After being given the menu, the cook brought the masala for those dishes on a plate to the ladies. They checked the quantities of herbs and spices, adding or removing from the plate if needed.

The cook bringing masala on a plate for approval is standard practice in our homes. Despite twenty years of training, Sabir, my cook, still checks the spices and their quantity with me before emptying them into the cooking utensil. For those who cook regularly, ingredients are measured only by *andaz*, a sense of proportion.

Abba with Nargis and Idrees uncle at Shama office

My father (right) with Raj Kapoor

The Golden Days

Shama Kothi was always filled with guests and we were often displaced from our bedrooms to accommodate an overflow. When we grumbled, Amma would say, '*Mehmaan to Allah ki rehmat hotey hain,*' guests are blessings from Allah. In Delhi's cultural tradition, Abba hosted mushairas, qawaali, music and literary gatherings followed by dinners. His graciousness earned Shama Kothi the reputation for *mahmaan nawazi,* hospitality, and for serving the finest of the city's cuisine.

Stalwarts of Urdu literature who wrote for *Shama* and *Sushma,* its Hindi version, visited our home. These included Ismat Chughtai, Qurratulain Haider, Kaifi Azmi, Sardar Jafri, Majrooh Sultanpuri, K.A. Abbas and Krishan Chander amongst others. I became friends with some of them. I was particularly close to Ainee Apa, Ismat Apa, Kaifi Sahab and Jafri Sahab. Lively conversations with them influenced my life in so many ways.

Many of these writers contributed poetry, essays and short stories for our magazines *Khilona, Bano,* an Urdu monthly journal

Golden nights at Shama Kothi

L-R: Phupijan, Ammi, Saira Banu, a guest, Ameena and Shamim Auntie at Shama Kothi

L-R: Daddy, Ammi, Shamim Auntie, Gulzar, Abba, Raakhee, Idrees and Ilyas uncle

for women, and *Shabistan*, a digest. Our other magazines included *Mujrim* and *Doshi*, popular crime digests in Urdu and Hindi.

In the seventies, my mother was the editor of *Bano*. I took over from her in the eighties and remained editor till the magazine closed in the early nineties. With my grandfather, both uncles and parents being writers, I grew up amidst newspapers, magazines, books and stationery. Newsprint, press and deadline, were among the first words that I learnt to say. The world of letters continues to be my refuge.

The magazine's film content was equally popular. Its film reviews affected box office results. *Shama* had a reputation for truthful reporting and often broke news about film stars. In the mid-fifties, Abba had begun to finance and distribute films. The distribution business was named after the magazine – Shama Distributors. In 1958, Abba financed and distributed the musical hit *Ghar Sansar*, with Nargis, Balraj Sahni and Rajendra Kumar. Films were regularly shown on portable screens on the lawn for family and friends.

Rajesh Khanna and Dimple lunching at Shama Kothi

Clockwise: *Bano*, 1969, *Shama* 1950s' editions

Growing up in an environment of literature and film was wonderful. When film personalities visited Delhi, Abba often hosted them. Our family was particularly close to Meena Kumari, Nimmi, Dilip Kumar, Raj Kapoor, Nargis, Saira Banu, Dev Anand, Dharmendra, Waheeda Rahman, Khwaja Ahmad Abbas, Kamal Amrohi, Mehboob Khan, K. Asif and others of that generation.

Meena Kumari stayed at Shama Kothi a few times. Nargis, with whom Abba shared a special friendship, visited us frequently. It was on Abba's insistence that Nargis agreed to work in *Raat aur Din*, produced by her brother. The film was released in 1967. Abba prevailed upon Sunil Dutt to allow Nargis to do the film, the only one she acted in after her marriage to him. Abba rightly predicted that she would receive the National Award for her performance. When Nargis became a Rajya Sabha member, Abba celebrated her nomination with a reception at Shama Kothi. On Nargis's death, Abba held a Quran *khwani,* recital, at the office and distributed food as ways of sending prayers for her soul. Both Sunil Dutt and Sanjay Dutt attended the memorial function.

Boarding school made us miss out on many of these glittering events. But I do remember Meena Kumari staying at our home and meeting Nargis, Nimmi and some other film personalities. I recall parties for newly married film couples. Rajesh and Dimple came home shortly after their wedding. They had first met at our Shama Film Awards function in Delhi. Raakhee and Gulzar also came home after their marriage. Abba gave the new brides an *asharfi*, gold guinea, as *moonh dikhaai*, gift money.

A decade after Abba's death, our magazines began to close down one by one due to the decline in Urdu readership in India, and these traditions too died. In 2002, Shama Kothi was sold. It was traumatic for us and we all wept on leaving that threshold forever. Tears still trickle down each time I drive past that road. Our house was bought by a political party, demolished and rebuilt. I caught a glimpse of an elephant statue where Amma's lemon trees once stood.

Jasmine and Jinns

My childhood memories are filled with the fragrance of *chameli,* jasmine, the most delicate of floral scents. Amma loved these little white flowers and had planted rows of jasmine shrubs all around our gardens. Delhi summers are synonymous with *motia* and *chameli* flowers. During the dry hot months, we slept under the starlit skies on the terrace. Each evening the terrace was hand-sprayed with water. Every family had a specific place for sleeping at night. Late afternoon, we helped Amma pluck the flowers. These had to be gathered before sunset for Amma said that flowers sleep at sundown.

Amma placed small bunches of jasmine on the chaarpai of the elders. These were taboo for us young girls. She warned that jinns are attracted to the fragrance of jasmine and if they smelled it on an unmarried girl they could become her *ashiq,* possessive lover. This would ruin their chances of getting married because many obstacles would arise.

Apa Saeeda narrated a story from her village of a young girl who went for an evening walk and never returned home. Her family looked everywhere but in vain. One day, they smelled an overpowering jasmine fragrance from a small *kothri,* storeroom, in a corner of the house. They found the missing girl there, and she told them that she had married a jinn and should be left alone. She asked them to forget her and advised them not to ever break or rebuild the house!

Everyone at Shama Kothi believed that jinns lived with us. Well after midnight, strange sounds would be heard. These resembled the creaking noise made when heavy furniture is moved. The same sounds were heard downstairs, upstairs and throughout the house for all the years that we lived there. There seemed no apparent reasons for this. The only explanation we came up with was that the jinns were dragging their beds in place before they slept. I guess we managed to coexist peacefully.

Sometimes these scary nocturnal banging sounds would awaken me from deep slumber. I would quietly creep into Apa Saeeda's bed. When I grew older, I simply got up, switched on the light and went back to sleep. Amma said we should not be scared because these were good jinns who had never caused us any harm. She said angels, jinns, humans, animals and birds were all part of God's creation. Allah created jinns from fire and human beings from clay. Jinns belonged to different faiths with both good and bad among them.

I do recall an occasional encounter with the jinns. One of our young cooks while making roti would suddenly stare at the sky and say, 'Salaam Alaikum' and faint. This strange behaviour continued for many days. Ammi then called a maulvi, who made the cook gaze into a candle flame. He apparently recognized the jinn who had been troubling him. The maulvi sahib then managed to successfully get rid of the jinn.

Amma said we couldn't see the jinns because they lived in another dimension. Jinns usually inhabit jungles, but sometimes their living areas overlap with humans. They have longer lives and travel at lightning speed, moving from anywhere to anywhere in the world in seconds. Jinns are known to be extreme in behaviour. This is why someone in a state of extreme rage is described as *jinaat bana hua hai*, he is behaving like a jinn.

As kids, we sat around Amma in her room, where a large area had a *dari chandni,* sheet covering, and *gau takya,* bolster cushions. She always wore a white hand embroidered kurta and duppatta. I loved her kurta buttons made of gold, embellished with precious stones. These buttons and diamond tops in her ears was the only jewellery she ever wore. She had a silver toothpick with a diamond pin head that was clipped to her kurta.

A silver paandaan in front of her, Amma cut *chaliya*, betel nuts with a *sarauta*, nut cutter, as she told us stories. Sometimes, she read us stories of Nastoor, the playful jinn, from *Khilona*. Most of the time these stories were of Prophets. I remember her telling us tales of Prophet Solomon, and how God endowed him with special gifts. All the jinns, animals and birds were made subservient to him. It is believed that the Prophet King constructed the temple at Jersualem, Dome of the Rock, with the help of jinns.

Badi Khala, my mother's elder sister, told us jinn anecdotes. She lived in Mohalla Baradari near Novelty Cinema. Strange and unusual incidents in her neighbour, Mariam Bi's house, had convinced them of the presence of jinns. They never harmed the family, but handwritten notes began to appear demanding specific food at odd hours! The poor woman had to make pakora or procure jalebi for them. Apparently the note would specify where to leave the food, usually on the terrace. It would soon disappear. Apart from food, the jinns liked film music and wanted certain songs to be played on the gramophone.

Tired of troublesome jinns, the family members discussed the idea of moving to another house. That night, a note appeared from nowhere threatening them with death if they left. The notes with strange messages kept appearing for a few weeks. Then one day a note apologizing for all the trouble appeared. The resident jinns said they had some guests who were just being mischievous. With that note and the departure of the guest jinns, the harassment stopped.

Most family elders had some jinn story or the other to narrate. Ammi remembers taps and doors opening on their own in the house where she spent her childhood. This was attributed to Muslim jinns doing their *wuzu*, ablutions, before offering prayers. She also recalls how once a wooden bed that her sister was sleeping on suddenly overturned. Their mother explained that the incident occurred because her sister's infant had soiled the bed. Impurities

Khilona magazine, 1971

are said to anger pious jinns, so a fresh sheet was quickly put in place of the soiled one.

In the mohallas, it is said that one should never close a *taq*, niche in the wall, because it blocks the passage for the jinns. Taq are typical of old style architecture. Phupijan, my father's younger sister, lived in one such house in Ballimaran, before selling it. The family that moved in suffered many misfortunes including a child falling off the terrace. They asked my aunt if a similar fate had ever struck them and she replied in the negative. Apparently, one of the family members then had a dream in which the jinns told them that they were angry at the taq being covered with cement. The cement layering was removed and the taq left open for the jinns to pass through.

Although the jinn population is believed to be more than that of humans, I don't hear jinn stories anymore. Maybe they have all moved to the mountains and jungles. I occasionally hear of mosques where jinns come to offer prayer. At dargahs, I often see men and women speaking and acting strangely while clinging to the trellis. It is presumed that they are possessed by a jinn and are probably trying to get rid of it.

During qawaali at dargah courtyards or in a *sama mehfil*, Sufi music gathering, a wide space is always left empty for the jinns. I have heard of instances when people blocking this space have been kicked and thrown off by invisible forces. It is said that jinns are extremely fond of Sufi music.

Amma died when I was thirteen years old and Shama Kothi was never the same. The pampering, the stories and everything came to an end. My father gave me her gold kurta buttons. Abba had jasmine shrubs planted over her grave. He visited her every Sunday and took the garderner along to tend to the jasmine. Fifteen years after Amma's death, Abba left us in the summer of 1985. He lies buried next to her with the waft of jasmine around their resting place.

Khatoon Begum, my Nani

My Nani from Karachi

I first met Nani, my maternal grandmother, when I was well into my teens. Till then she was a faceless Khatoon Begum who lived in Karachi. Nana, my maternal grandfather, died long before I was born. They had eleven children, of whom seven survived, my mother was the youngest of them. In 1960, Nani moved to Karachi to join her brothers who had migrated there after Partition. Two of her daughters had also migrated to Karachi with their husbands.

Nani visited Delhi occasionally, her last trip was in October 1983. She was not keeping well, so Ammi sent me to Karachi to help with the Indian visa and escort her to Delhi. Nani's visa was valid for ninety days and I had submitted her passport to the home ministry for an extension. The need for an extension never arose because Nani left us exactly on the ninetieth day of her stay. She died peacefully in her sleep at our home, surrounded by her children and grandchildren. As fate would have it, after thirty years of Nana's death, there lay a vacant grave adjacent to his. We laid her to rest there in Sheedipura, the centuries old community graveyard near Idgah. As death beckoned, Nani's ancestral city embraced her.

Nani was a strong independent woman and I enjoyed her humour, sarcasm and stories. While in Delhi, she divided her time between the families of her two daughters and two sons. Ammi worried as she often took off on her own, roaming the city using public transport. She would reassure Ammi, showing her the *pudiya*, small packet, of red chilli powder that she secretly carried under her white cotton burqa. She said if anyone dared harass her, they would be blinded with chillies! She even slept with red chilli powder under her pillow and advised me to do the same.

Nani had a colourful vocabulary and used many old *muhavarey*, proverbs. She defined a sharp-tongued girl as a *hari mirch*, green chilli. If someone described a girl as simple and she thought otherwise,

Nani would retort, *'Jalebi ki tarha seedhi hai,'* meaning the girl was as straight as a jalebi! Describing someone's luxurious life, Nani would say, *'Paanchon ungliyan ghee mai, sar kadhai mai,'* the whole hand and head is dipped in ghee.

Nani was generally distrustful of people and disapproved of the younger female domestic staff at home. She warned Ammi that with men in the house, this should be avoided. Girls with unconventional, sultry attractive features were described as *namkeen chehra*, salty face. Nani worried that one of these women was more than just attractive, describing her as *namak ki bori*, a sack of salt.

Nani once tried to convince her young, handsome grandson to get married but he showed no interest. Having heard of his girlfriends, with a twinkle in her eye, Nani said, *'Cut piece mil raha hai toh thaan kyoon khareedey ga,'* if cut pieces are available, why would you purchase whole yard of cloth! This expression became a favourite family joke. Bothered by my younger brother's wild crop of hair and faded jeans, she would question his *'Beetal aur huppy,'* Beatles and hippy look. Before I met Nani, I addressed my mother as 'Mummy'. Offended, she made me say Ammi, because *'mummy to Qahra key ajaib ghar mai hoti hai,'* mummies are in Cairo museum.

Nani was rather eccentric, particularly when it came to food. We often joked about her peculiarities, but agreed that it rewarded her with a long and healthy life. She ate only vegetables that grew above the ground and not those that ripened under the soil. Nani also discouraged us from eating potatoes, turnip and arvi. She said they burdened the digestive system. Her diet consisted of vegetables, such as ghiya, turaiyan, bhindi and other greens. While cooking these vegetables with meat, Nani used spices in small quantities with abundant shorba. Health took priority over taste. All of Nani's children, including my mother, became almost obsessed with health food. Ammi still prefers stir fried vegetable to biryani and qorma.

Nani referred to *baingan*, brinjal, as *begun*, worthless. Some consider brinjal to be a rich source of iron, but not her. She never touched the vegetable saying, 'Pet mai pada rahega,' it stays in the stomach forever. Vegetables like baingan, kaddu and kathal are alien to our cooking.

Nani did not enjoy mithai and would encourage her brood to eat fruits instead. Ammi did the same with us siblings. My health-conscious mother's mantra remains 'milk and fruit'. Even now, she mostly skips dinner and has a glass of hot milk with a spoonful of honey instead. As kids, snacking on parantha, samosa, chole bhature, tikki and golgappa remained taboo. So, I just never developed a taste for them.

When in Delhi, Nani avoided drinking tap water. She was convinced that the Jamuna waters were polluted. To cater to the needs of a large family, a bore well had been dug at Shama Kothi. Nani drank water from this well and when staying elsewhere, carried water from our house.

Nani always washed vegetables with potassium permanganate, oxidizing crystals that were called 'pinky' because of the pinkish colour they acquired on mixing with water. I recently read that health experts advise the same to get rid of pesticides and toxins. When I informed Ammi of this news, she said, 'Well, my mother always knew that.'

If someone fell sick, Nani had a home remedy for it. Those complaining of headaches were advised to sit in the morning sun and eat jalebi made in desi ghee. A running tummy could be cured with sabudana. This would be cooked with a tablespoon of milk to make it edible. Ammi and I use this remedy and it works like magic. At the end of each meal, Nani munched a few whole mint leaves saying it helped in cleansing the liver. She also chewed a few white peppercorns to aid digestion. As much as possible, I try following the wisdom of Nani's teachings.

Early Lessons

Our elders told us that the best food is the food shared with others, for it brings barakat, blessings to the table. Prior to eating or drinking anything, we were made to recite 'Bismillah ir-Rahman -ir-Rahim,' In the name of Allah, Most Merciful, Most Compassionate.

Apa Saeeda taught us on how to eat using three fingers of the right hand. No leftovers could remain on the plate. Daddy's plate looked so clean after the meal that Ammi would blemish it with a little curry. She worried that it if it looked like an unused plate, it could be left unwashed. Apa Saeeda repeatedly said that leftovers find their way to the shaitan, devil's, stomach. I feared leaving food on the plate because it would make me responsible for energizing the devil!

After meals, Apa Saeeda collected the leftover roti. While chatting, Amma and Apa Saeeda broke these into fine crumbs, and sprinkled them on the lawns for the birds. Leftover meat was fed to the cats that roamed around the house. Bones were collected from the plates and left on the street for the dogs. No food item was trashed in the garbage. Apa Saeeda warned that on Qayamat, the Day of Judgement, God would take us to account for every wasted morsel.

The same warning applied to water. Apa Saeeda never allowed us leisurely baths, wasting water was a strict no. She said water is a form of Allah's Mercy, and explained, 'Ek ek boond ka hisaab dena padey ga,' you will be accountable for every drop of wasted water. Her lessons about water consciousness have made me cautious with its use.

The elders reprimanded us for drinking water while standing or in a single gulp, 'Ghataghat paani nahin peetey, teen baar main peetey hain aur baith kar peetey hain,' don't gulp down water, sit down and sip it with three breaks. Some years ago, my acupressure therapist told me that one must always drink water while sitting and never in a single gulp. He seemed surprised when I told him that this is what we always did.

Amongst other lessons, we were told never to criticize food as it was risq, provision, from Allah. When the elders thought the quality of food served to them was not good, they simply said, '*Bas, Allah deta rahey*,' may Allah continue to provide! On the rare occasion that Abba thought some dish did not taste right, he just said, '*Omelette bana do*,' make me an omelette. This was enough to send the whole household in a panic.

A tradition that has been lost is placing the food on the table before the bread. Nowadays, not many are even aware of this nuance. Amma made sure that on festive occasions, and even during daily meals, the food was bought to the table before the roti. On occasions of mourning, the roti had to be placed first. This symbolizes *tukda todna*, breaking bread, and grieving together.

Other table rules included washing our hands but not wiping them before meals. We had to offer a short thanksgiving prayer before the table was cleared. We were told to take food from the side of the dish and not dig into the centre as it held the blessings. Tasting a bit of everything served on the table was another lesson. All these rules come from the *Sunnah*, normative practices of Prophet Muhammad ﷺ. These are taught to Muslim children from a young age so that they turn into lifelong habits.

Kebab stalls on the steps of the Jama Masjid
Photo: Vaseem Ahmed Dehlvi

The Halal Word

The Islamic ruling of staying away from pork and eating only halal meat was taught to us early in life. It is permissible to consume the meat of most non-predatory animals. All kinds of fishes are halal except those which died in the sea without any apparent external cause. The halal process requires that animals be alive and healthy before the slaughter. Meat becomes halal when the name of Allah is pronounced while putting the knife to the animal's jugular. The blood must be drained from the carcass, as blood is haram. While on *shikar*, hunt, devout Muslims ensure that their hunt does not die before the halal process. If that occurs, the meat is haram.

These rules are passed on from one generation to another. I must have taught my son the rule about not eating pork when he was just old enough to differentiate between animals. Once, when he was about six years old and harassing me, I told him to keep quiet and angrily called him a *suar*, swine. He began to wail loudly and uncontrollably. Infuriated, I asked 'What is it now?' In between sobs, he said, 'You have called me the name of an animal that we are not even allowed to eat!' I had to apologise, kiss and make up, resolving never to use the word again.

Since Jewish dietary rules are quite similar to Islamic requirements, we were allowed kosher food. My father always advised me to order kosher food while travelling on an international airline. When invited for meals to the homes of non-Muslim friends, I pretend to be a vegetarian citing health concerns. Sensing my discomfort, sometimes the hosts assure me that the meat has been bought from a Muslim butcher. Much to the shock of some friends, when eating out in a restaurant I regularly enquire if the meat is halal. If the answer is vague, I stick to eating vegetables or fish.

Interestingly, lobster, crab, prawn and other shellfish are permissible by Islamic dietary rules, but fall in the *makrooh*, not

A food stall in Nizamuddin Basti

preferred, category. Most Muslims don't seem to be bothered by this category. There is no prohibition on beef consumption. However, pertaining to the meat of cow and buffalo, Prophet Muhammad ﷺ did famously say, 'There is value in its milk, healing in its ghee, and a disease in its meat.' He never ate beef nor did he encourage it. I know many Sufi masters and family elders who refrain from eating beef because of these Prophetic norms.

The word halal is not just about the way food is processed. It has a more profound meaning that confirms to Islamic values of morality and integrity.

Kakori kebab from Al Kauser

Ammi, Vaseem and I

Ammi and I

Ammi has no interest in cooking. Luckily, she never had to deal with daily kitchen chores. The youngest of eleven siblings, and the eldest bahu of the Dehlvi *khandaan*, family, there was no pressure to cook in either home. Her interests lay in writing, designing garments and handicrafts for her export house. A non-conformist, Ammi never understood why women's hands should smell of garlic and ginger. She maintains that only women with oppressive husbands become good cooks.

Although a food connoisseur, Daddy never complained about food. He still makes claims about being able to differentiate between food that has been cooked on a gas stove from that which has been cooked on wooden logs. He yearns for the dal his mother cooked in a clay pot on wood.

While friends and family are appreciative of my cooking, Ammi is not. She rebukes me saying, '*Mai ney tumko khana pakaney ke liye nahin padhaya likhaya*,' I did not educate you to waste your time in the kitchen. Ammi thinks most women cook well and that it does not count as a great achievement.

I guess I can never say, 'No one cooks like my mother,' as she still has trouble boiling rice and preparing basic dal. She rarely goes into the kitchen and does not know any traditional recipes. However, just like most people in our community, she understands our cuisine to the last detail. Ammi remains my severest critic and the hardest to please. Food must look *khushrang*, inviting, because *pehle aankh khaati hai*, first the eyes feast on the food. The aroma must be seductive and the meat and vegetables should be done just right, with no single spice overpowering the other. Be it garlic, onion, salt or ginger, everything must be used in its correct proportion and the garnishing must be perfect. If a dish requires mint leaves for garnishing, you cannot replace them with coriander leaves!

Ammi and I keep disagreeing about the oil and salt content in the food. I tend to use minimum oil and salt. On being told that too much salt is not good for health, Ammi wants to know if I cooked for her or hospital patients. I hate to admit that other than the salt factor, Ammi is mostly right in her criticism. I breathe a sigh of relief on that rare occasion when she gives a nod of approval. I know then that the cooking has been marked ten on ten.

I first began cooking while living in New York during the year 1978. Missing comfort food, I managed to rustle up decent meals. Watching Apa Saeeda in the kitchen while growing up helped. I often spoke to her on the phone and wrote recipes down. My friends enjoyed my experiments with cooking and their responses encouraged me to work harder in the kitchen.

I found New York's food kiosks and street food culture fascinating. This inspired me to create an eatery when I returned to Delhi. In 1979, Ammi and I founded Al Kauser, named after her middle name. For many years, this remained the sole roadside kiosk outside the old city to sell kebab, tikka, biryani and qorma. It is located at the corner of Sardar Patel Marg and Malcha Marg, just across where Shama Kothi used to be. The large open area adjoining my bedroom was converted into a kitchen. Al Kauser became particularly famous for its kakori kabab. I created our signature dish by wrapping a kebab in a chappati and named it 'wrap a kebab'. The phrase caught on and is still used in dhabas and eateries across the city to refer to the ubiquitous kebab roll. I went back to writing and it was Ammi's day-to-day supervision that turned Al Kauser into a success story.

The kakori kebab were made by Ishtiaq Qureshi from Kakori, a small town near Lucknow. He came from a family that specialized in the art of making these melt-in-the-mouth kebabs. Ammi knew Ishtiaq and convinced him to work at Al Kauser. Ishtiaq then worked as chief assistant to the acclaimed Imtiaz Qureshi, then the head chef at Maurya Sheraton. One of the reasons he agreed to join us was that he enjoyed interacting with customers who appreciated his craft rather than work inside a hotel kitchen. He moved in with his family and stayed in the staff quarters. Ishtiaq died many years ago, but his son Ashfaq continues to manage the kiosk successfully. Al Kauser now has a branch in Vasant Place Market near Vasant Vihar. The kebab are still the best in town.

Although not a foodie, I have always enjoyed having family and friends over for meals. Keeping Abba's tradition alive, I often hosted evenings of Urdu poetry and qawaali at Shama Kothi. Ammi helped organize the dinners that followed the mehfil and food was ordered from the professional cooks in the old city. These days, the best known of them is Hakim, from Gali Rodgran near Ballimaran. On festive occasions, we often order biryani, qorma and other traditional dishes from him.

In my early thirties, I married Reza Perwaiz, who came from Ambari that falls in Azamgargh district in Uttar Pradesh. God bless Reza's soul, he was extremely finicky about food. In many ways, his fussiness improved my cooking. With Reza, each dal had to have the traditional bhagar. As with most UPwalas, arhar dal was his favourite. It had to have a bhagar of *lasan ke sabut javey*, browned whole pods of garlic. He did not enjoy fusion or Punjabi food. Everything had to be made in a traditional or continental style. He would scorn at the mere thought of kadhai chicken, butter chicken and makhani dal. An erstwhile tea planter and a bit of a brown sahib, he relished cutlet, chicken roast and caramel custard.

Reza and I often clashed over the Delhi and UP methods of cooking. He loved aloo qeema, which we don't make. He preferred khichda over haleem. When cooking vegetables, UPwalas chop them into tiny pieces, while we cut them slightly larger. Even these little details mattered a great deal. Our son Arman, often got caught up in this age old ongoing tussle between UP and Delhi of supermacy regarding cuisine. Ultimately, the Dehlvi in him prevailed. One of

My New York days

The opening of Al Kauser in 1979

the dishes Reza taught me to prepare was khili safed mash ki dal, dry white lentil, which became a great hit. I am not sharing this recipe as it is a UP specialty, and perhaps I should keep a few recipes secret!

Gone are the when I could invite over any number of guests to Shama Kothi without having to worry about a thing. Now that I live in a flat, there are concerns of space at home and parking. However, on a much smaller scale, I make the effort to maintain family traditions. I keep an open house and enjoy having friends and family stay over. I try to ensure that no one leaves my home without being fed, be it the guests or their drivers, the caprenter or tailor. Thankfully, with friends dropping in all the time, it is rare that Arman and I are alone at the dining table. This is one of the blessings in our lives.

With some dish or the other being prepared, the kitchen is the most active part of my home. I am paranoid about running out of provisions and keep a large stock. For the last few years, my life in the kitchen is increasingly about niaz and langar. With help from Sabir, I personally prepare food for langar.

Niaz, offering of food, that we make at home generally consists of aloo salan, chicken qorma or yakhni pulao and mithai. After a short prayer, some of this *tabaruk*, blessed, langar is shared at home and rest is distributed to the needy. I offer niaz on various days of the Islamic calendar marking special days in the life of the Prophet Muhammad ﷺ and his family, Khwaja Moinuddin Chishti, Hazrat Nizamudin Auliya and some other Sufis whom I deeply love. Sometimes, we celebrate these occasions with a qawaali at home. Thanks to Dhruv Sangari, my friend and wonderful Sufi singer, hosting a mehfil has become easy. Bless him, he never never turns down my request. After the music, we serve food on a typical Dilli yellow coloured, cotton printed dastarkhwan on the floor over the white chandni, with guests sitting on both sides. These Sufi traditions keep my soul nourished.

Al Kauser: The kebab kiosk
Ammi and I established

With a son who is a singer and his group of talented friends who play the guitar, flute, and various other instruments, we also get to listen to some brilliant classical and contemporary music. Sometimes, it gets a little crowded, which is even more delightful.

When planning a mehfil, I keep a simple menu with one mutton gravy dish, a chicken or mutton yakhni pulao, dahi badey, a seasonal vegetable dish and a dal. I prefer making a few good dishes rather than serving a large variety of food. If vegetarians are expected, I make matar pulao as well and add another vegetable or two. More often than not, these music evenings happen spontaneously. Then it is just a potluck dinner.

Having trained Sabir over the years, thankfully I don't have to cook every day. On special occasions, I supervise the cooking. Standing in the kitchen during the Delhi summer is tough, but in winter I enjoy spending time near the stove. I like to shop for vegetables, fruits and spices myself, but don't always have the time.

I usually buy fruit from Bhogul and vegetables from Barapullah, the dilapidated seventeenth-century bridge from the Mughal era, which comes alive each evening with vendors. Both these markets are close to my home. Once every few months, I go to Khari Baoli to replenish my stock of spices. I buy mostly from Mehar Chand, a shop that has been around for over a hundred years. The coriander and red chilli powder in my kitchen are from Shan-e-Delhi, a local brand. I get these from shops in the Nizamuddin Basti. I buy fresh mutton and chicken from Indian Traders in Gole Market. They have been supplying meat, chicken and fish to my family for more than thirty years. They know how finicky we are about meat and cuts. Good quality meat, vegetables, spices, some effort and a little love thrown in make all the difference in food.

Spices in Khari Baoli Market, Delhi

Essential Herbs and Spices

Ginger, whole
Ginger paste
Garlic, whole
Garlic paste
Coriander powder
Coriander seeds
Red chilli, whole
Red chilli powder
Deghi mirch
Turmeric powder (haldi)
Black cardamom (badi elaichi)
Green cardamom (choti elaichi)
Cumin seeds (zeera)
Peppercorns (kaali mirch)
Cinnamon sticks (dalchini)
Cloves (laung)
Dried ginger (sonth)
Bay leaves (tezpata)
Garam masala
Fenugreek seeds (methi dana)
Carom seeds (ajwain)
Nigella seeds (kalonji)
Poppy seeds (khush khaash)
Fennel seeds (saunf)
Nutmeg (jaiphal)
Mace (javitri)
Saffron (zafran)
Kewra water
Vegetable oil
Desi ghee
Salt

The kitchen shelves of a typical Dilliwala are well stocked, containing spices in large jars. One of the basic ingredients for *salan*, meat curries, is *lal pyaaz*, golden fried onions. Since lal pyaaz is constantly required, we slice the onions, fry and dry them out on paper towels. These are stored in air-tight jars without any refrigeration and remain usable for weeks. Keeping fried onions ready cuts cooking time by almost half. The colour of the onions must be a perfect golden brown or else the colour, flavour and taste of the dish will be affected adversely. Slicing onions finely in half circles and deep-frying them to the right colour is truly an art. I have now begun to keep packets of ready to use crisp Fried Onions by Lazeez, a Delhi-based brand. Their quality is good and they and fried to the perfect colour for our kind of food.

Curd is another ingredient added to almost all meat preparations. Most of us usually make curd at home. One of the major differences in the Punjabi method of cooking and the Dilliwala method is the use of curd. Punjabi food is largely tomato based and our food is curd based. Tomatoes are used sparingly and are added to a few meat dishes and vegetable preparations. Curd enhances the flavour of the meat and spices in a subtle way whereas tomatoes have an overpowering effect on both colour and taste.

The quality of herbs and spices is the key to any good cooking. Traditionally, all spices were grounded at home. Some of my cousins still grind chilli powder and coriander powder themselves. Growing up, I watched Amma taking great pains to have whole masalas washed, dried and ground. There was never any question of using readymade chilli and coriander powder. Modern lifestyles don't allow for such indulgences anymore, so one depends on what is available in the market.

When travelling in India or foreign lands, my friends often request me to rustle up meals. While I cook, many take lessons and write down recipes. I find that in most homes, garlic and ginger paste is mixed and put in a single jar. We would never do this. Garlic and ginger paste should be stored separately because they are used in different quantities. Besides, their flavours should be kept from overlapping. In almost all meat preparations, the quantity of garlic used is slightly larger than the ginger. Some dishes don't need ginger at all, while others require shredded ginger. Ideally, it is best to prepare fresh ginger and garlic paste.

Food traditionalists don't use the pressure cooker, preferring to cook on low flame. However, I must confess to relying on modern methods to save time. With the help of a pressure cooker, it takes no more than twenty odd minutes to prepare dishes like aloo salan, qorma or mutton stew. I even use the pressure cooker for preparing the meat base for yakhni pulao and biryani!

Lal pyaaz, golden fried onions

Degh of biryani and qorma

Some All-Time Favourites

Biryani, yakhni pulao, stew, shaami kebab, qeema and qorma are amongst the most popular dishes cooked all through the year. Aloo salan, or aloo gosht as it is sometimes called, is an all-time favourite. Over the last decade or so, it has replaced the traditional mutton qorma at wedding banquets.

I have heard elders recall, how in the old days, serving aloo salan at weddings would have been deemed as an insult. Mamoo Abdullah said that in earlier times, the *baraat*, groom's marriage party, would have taken offence and gone back without the bride had they been served aloo salan! This is because the dish was *maute ka khana*, food served at post-funeral gatherings.

When non-Muslim friends come to Muslim homes, they expect to be fed qorma, biryani and kebab. So, one must live up to the reputation! Personally, I prefer yakhni pulao to biryani as its flavour is much more nuanced. When required in large quantities, biryani is ordered from professional cooks who make it in a degh. Pulaos are usually accompanied with varieties of chutneys and pickles. Yakhni pulao is ideally had with arq-e-nana chutney, which is sweet. In summer, it is accompanied with simple raita, beaten curd with a sprinkling of salt and pepper. Yakhni literally means broth or stock. Since the rice is cooked in meat stock, it is called yakhni pulao.

Biryani is traditionally not cooked in meat stock. Rice is parboiled separately with certain herbs and spices. Then the rice and meat are layered with the *adkachra*, half-done, meat. In addition to the Dilli biryani, other popular biryani include the Hyderabadi, Sindhi, Bohri and Awadhi variety.

Professional cooks use the sella variety of rice for biryani as it does not break easily. For home cooking, basmati is preferred. Basmati rice is lighter on the stomach and the *khushboo*, aroma, is fantastic. I learnt an easy-to-cook biryani recipe from my cousin

Qurratulain. Khala Rabia named her after the acclaimed Urdu writer Qurratulain Haider and like her, she got nicknamed Ainee. She is the family MasterChef who sends me mouth-watering chutneys, murabba and achaar.

Biryani, pulao, qorma and stew are made with both chicken and mutton. Dilliwalas prefer mutton, but now that mutton costs around ₹500 a kg, it is more economical to use chicken. Besides the cost factor, chicken is gaining popularity as people are getting health conscious and prefer white meats. Frankly, the broiler chickens one gets these days have little taste. *Desi*, free range organic chicken, taste wonderful but are not readily available. If ordered specially from the supplier, they cost more than mutton.

Qeema, mincemeat, is another all-time favourite and one can whip up so many different varieties of qeema. Dilliwalas are very exacting about the quality of the mincemeat. My mother says, 'Never ever trust a butcher with qeema and always have it made in front of you.' My driver Abdul, whom I send for this purpose, has strict instructions to stand guard while it is being minced.

Ammi says that the minute your eyes evade the butcher, he could add the *chichdey*. She reminds me of the adage, '*Qasai chichdey zaroor dalega aur darzi apni ma ke kafan se bhi kapda bacha lega,*' a butcher cannot resist adding scraps of inedible meat and tailors will ensure they save some cloth even from their mother's shroud!

The best way to buy qeema is to purchase the whole raan, leg, and get the butcher to mince the meat under supervision. I follow this rule, even though the qeema cost increases. I keep the bones separately and use them for soup stock. Dilliwalas generally don't use qeema minced with machine and prefer *haath ka kutta hua qeema*, manually minced meat. Butchers fuss about it as this takes more of their time. But if you are a regular customer, they will take the trouble.

Masala for salan

Aloo Salan – Potatoes with Meat

I begin the recipes with aloo gosht – or as we call it, aloo salan – the most popular dish on my table. No party at home is complete without it. Friends crave aloo salan and I find myself sharing the recipe all the time. The potatoes soaked in the masala and shorba makes them taste different from other varieties of cooked potatoes.

Ideally, the potatoes should be of medium size. I handpick potatoes becuase the uniformity in size makes the dish look appealing. Potatoes are sliced lengthwise into two halves. If the potatoes are not sliced the correct way, one can tell that the cook is a novice.

½ kg mutton
5–6 potatoes
4–5 medium-sized onions, golden fried
2 tsp garlic paste
1½ tsp ginger paste

1½-2 tsp red chilli powder

3-4 tbsp coriander powder

4 cloves (laung)

2 black cardamom pods

6 green cardamoms

200 gm curd

1 cup oil

Salt to taste

Heat oil and add the green and black cardamom pods and cloves. After a minute, add chilli powder, garlic and ginger paste, coriander powder and salt. It's best to put all this masala on a plate and then add with a little water, maybe a quarter of a cup. The water ensures that the masala does not burn. After a minute or two, when the masala is lightly fried and the oil bubbles rise, add the mutton. Stirring occasionally, leave on medium or high flame for 5 to 10 minutes. Keep the cooking vessel open so that the water released from the meat evaporates as does its *bisand*, odour. Meanwhile, blend the fried onions and the curd together for a few seconds in the mixer and keep it aside.

Once the meat is slightly cooked, and the oil is bubbling, add the blended onion and curd mixture to the meat. The secret of smooth gravy is this blended mixture. Keep on medium flame for 5 to 10 minutes to *bhuno,* cook the curd. When oil bubbles rise, add 2 cups of water for the gravy. The level of the water should be a few inches above the meat. If you are going to use the pressure cooker, then you could add a little more water.

I rely on the pressure cooker for aloo salan, allowing one whistle for the meat. When the cooker cools, check the meat, which should be half done. Now add the potatoes and close the cooker. The potatoes and meat should be done with one more whistle. If cooking on low flame without a cooker, keep a check on the meat. When it is half done, add the potatoes and cook till both are cooked.

Garnish with fresh chopped coriander leaves and a sprinkling of garam masala.

Khadey Masaley ka Qorma – Mutton Stew

Old Dilliwalas often call khadey masaley ka qorma 'istew', a corruption of the English word stew. It most likely has its origins in British India, inspired by the English version of the mutton stew. It was Nani Amma's favourite dish, and one with which she demonstrated her cooking prowess. Ammi, too, loves stew, probably because of this association. Thankfully, it is one of the dishes I make that meets her standards.

Mutton stew is one of the simplest dishes to prepare. Once you have the ingredients ready, everything is literally put in together. Because of the variety of spices used, the aroma is just divine.

1 kg mutton
300 gm curd
5-6 medium-sized onions, sliced into four
1 tsp turmeric powder
4-5 black cardamom pods
6-8 cloves
3-4 tsbp coriander seeds, fresh crushed
6-8 red chillies, whole
2-3" cinnamon
8-10 black peppercorns
2 medium-sized tomatoes, chopped
2 tbsp garlic, finely chopped
2 tbsp ginger, finely chopped
2-3 bay leaves
1 cup oil
Salt to taste

Stew is easy to make as it does not need monitoring at every stage. All the ingredients are put in the cooking utensil together and left on low flame till done. The curd and tomatoes take care of the gravy and it doesn't need extra water. Stew should not be very watery. I usually pressure-cook the stew for two whistles and then cook further till excess water has dried. Sometimes, I add a topping of desi ghee to enhance the aroma.

Chicken Stew

Although stew is traditionally made with mutton, you can use the above recipe for chicken stew. Be careful as chicken gets done quickly. It is best to fry the chicken for a few minutes before adding the rest of the spices. The frying hardens the skin and prevents the chicken pieces from breaking while cooking. And never, ever cook chicken in a pressure cooker.

Qorma

1 kg mutton or chicken
5-6 medium-sized onions, golden fried
2 tsp garlic paste
1½ tsp ginger paste
1 tsp red chilli powder
1 tsp deghi mirch
4 tsp coriander powder
6 cloves
6 peppercorns
400 gm curd
¼ tsp crushed nutmeg (jaiphal)
¼ tsp crushed mace (javitri)
10–12 almonds (optional)
1 tsp kewra water (optional)
10 green cardamoms

1-1½ cup oil

Salt to taste

Heat oil and fry meat along with garlic and ginger paste for 5 to 10 minutes till oil bubbles rise. Now add 5 green cardamoms, chilli powder, coriander powder, almond paste, cloves, nutmeg and mace, peppercorns, salt and curd to the meat. The deghi mirch adds a deep red colouring.

Another method is to add all these ingredients with the curd, mix them well and then add to the meat. Continue to fry the meat for 5 to 10 minutes till the oil rises. Now add 2-3 cups of water for the gravy. Cover and leave on low flame till almost done.

Now handcrush the golden fried onions into tiny pieces. Do not use a blender as crushing by hand ensures the *danedar*, coarse, thick texture of the gravy. Lastly, add crushed onions, crushed cardamoms and kewra to the meat. Cover and leave on low flame for another 5 to 10 minutes till the meat is tender.

Note: If you want the qorma gravy to be smoother, blend the fried onions and curd together for a few seconds in mixer.

Yakhni Pulao

Biryani has its origins in Delhi, whereas pulao was perfected in Awadh. Whatever the origins of the yakhni pulao, it is enjoyed and cooked in our homes. The meat traditionally used in yakhni pulao is mutton breast, because the *chiknai,* fat, enhances the taste. Personally, I prefer lean meat and use a mixture of mutton cuts for pulao. Long grain basmati rice gives the best results.

If making chicken pulao, simply replace the mutton with the chicken. Traditionally, the quantity of meat is almost double of that of the rice. Chicken pulao is one of the few chicken dishes I make regularly and recommend.

½ kg basmati rice

¾ kg mutton or chicken

10–12 peppercorns

5–6 cloves

4 pods black cardamom

2" cinnamon

4–5 bay leaves

1 tbsp cumin seeds

4–5 medium-sized onions, sliced

2 tsp garlic paste

1 tsp ginger paste

4–6 tbsp ginger strips, finely chopped

1 cup oil

Salt to taste

Leave the rice soaked in water for 30 to 45 minutes. Heat oil and fry the onion slices for about 5 to 10 minutes till translucent. Take care that the onion does not turn brown, or else you will have a slightly brownish pulao.

When the onions are done, add all the spices except the ginger strips. Fry for a minute or two and add the meat pieces. Fry the meat till the water released from it has evaporated, and oil bubbles appear. Then add about 3-4 cups of water and let the meat cook. If using mutton, you could use a pressure cooker for one whistle. Chicken cannot be pressure cooked; it just needs 10 to 15 minutes on a low flame. Cook the meat till it is nearly done.

Now, add the soaked rice to the meat along with the ginger strips. Check the level of water. The rule is *do ungal* above the meat, which means that if you were to dip your finger in the cooking vessel, the water should cover the second marking on your index finger. It would roughly be about 2" above the meat. Add a little more water if needed. Cook on medium flame till the rice absorbs the water and then minimize the flame and leave for about 15 to 20 minutes till the rice is done. When making biryani and pulao, we usually place a cloth before putting the lid, and then place a weight on the lid. This is to ensure that the steam doesn't escape, so both the rice and meat cook well. It is called *dam dena*.

Matar Pulao – Green Pea Pulao

For matar pulao, just follow the yakhni pulao recipe; merely replacing the meat with ¾ kg shelled green peas. Using the same spices lends a unique flavour to it.

At the risk of sounding arrogant, I must say that the matar pulao cooked in our homes is extraordinary. It is generally cooked in winter with fresh green peas. However, with frozen peas available, the pulao makes for a wholesome dish any time of the year. I cook it regularly, particularly for serving vegetarian guests. Matar pulao is best served with shalgam ka achaar, which is made with turnips, a few spices and water. It is somewhat like the Punjabi *kanji*, yet different. At the beginning of winter, one of the first food items that Dilliwalas make is this water-based achaar, without which matar pulao is just not acceptable!

Biryani

Everybody loves a good biryani. It is invariably associated with a dinner or banquet hosted by Muslims. The Sindhis, Bohras, Hyderabadis and others have their own versions of the biryani, which are becoming popular. Readymade masala mixes from Pakistan help you produce wonderful Sindhi biryani. However, I believe our biryani is the ultimate, especially the biryani cooked by professionals that is served at weddings and other occasions. Dilliwalas have a couple of different recipes for biryani, but I am going to reveal the easiest home version.

I don't remember eating chicken biryani in my childhood, for biryani was traditionally made with mutton. However, in the last decade or so, chicken biryani has become quite popular, even at weddings. I think the rising cost of mutton is the reason for the changeover. Chicken biryani tastes good but, frankly, it doesn't come close to the original mutton biryani.

Traditionally, the ratio of meat used in biryani is *ded guna*, which is one-and-a-half times the quantity of the rice. In the old days, saffron was used but with good quality saffron difficult to find, most of us use food colouring. If you add saffron, then nothing like it. Earlier, haarsingar flowers, called night jasmine in English, were soaked in water that was added to biryani for colouring and fragrance. Women used the remaining water to colour their dupattas. Commonly used in ayurvedic and unani medicine, these flowers are sold at about ₹3,000 a kilogram in some shops in the old city.

¾ kg mutton or chicken
½ kg basmati rice
2 tsp garlic
1½ tsp ginger
10 green cardamoms
8 cloves
300 gm curd
¾ cup oil or desi ghee
½ cup milk
2 tsp kewra water
½ tsp saffron or saffron colour
1 cup desi ghee or oil
Salt to taste

Soak the basmati rice for 30 to 45 minutes. Heat oil, add 4 cloves and 5 green cardamoms and leave for a minute or two. Cardamoms are best when slightly crushed. Add the garlic, ginger, salt and meat, frying for a few minutes. Add the curd and continue frying till the oil separates from the meat. Now add about 2-3 cups water, and pressure-cook for one whistle. Or let the meat cook on slow flame till the meat is three-fourth done.

Now add the soaked rice along with the remaining 4 cloves and
5 cardamoms to the meat. The water in the utensil should remain
about 2½" above the rice. Add a little more water if necessary. Cook
on medium flame, when the water is absorbed, then minimize the
flame. Now, mix the saffron or saffron colouring with milk and
pour around the rice. Sprinkle the kewra over it as well.

Place a thick cloth or small towel over the utensil before placing
the lid. Leave on dum for 10 to 15 minutes till the rice and meat
are done. One of the signs of a good biryani is that the rice should
not be overcooked. Each grain of rice should remain separate from
the other.

Kofta – Meat Balls in Gravy

Kofta is a bit tricky to make and needs a little practice. So don't be
disillusioned if you don't get them right in the first attempt. Since
kofta require fine mincemeat, the butcher needs to be informed so
that he makes the meat accordingly. In our families, when getting
meat for koftas, ingredients such as green chillies, onions, fresh
coriander leaves are sent to the butcher to add to the meat in the
mincing process. Kofta are cooked throughout the year and a great
hit with everyone, particularly with those who prefer boneless meat.

One of the ingredients used in kofta is *khush khaash*, poppy seeds.
I know some people who got into serious trouble with customs in
Saudi Arabia for carrying poppy seeds. The Arabs refused to believe
that they were meant for cooking. They just see poppy as a form
of drugs! I learnt how to make kofta from Asiya, Khala Rabia's
younger daughter.

Kofta

½ kg fine mincemeat
2 green chillies, finely chopped
½ tsp poppy seeds

3 tbsp roasted chana, powdered

3 tbsp curd (optional)

2 medium-sized onions, finely chopped

1 tsp garam masala

1 tbsp oil or desi ghee

25 gm fresh coriander leaves, finely chopped

Salt to taste

It is best to grind all the ingredients in a blender and mix with mincemeat. Now make small round balls by gently rolling the mince in your palms. Wet your hands before making the kofta. You can make 12-14 small koftas with ½ kg of mincemeat.

Gravy

4 medium-sized onions, golden fried

200–250 gm curd

1 tsp garlic paste

4–5 tsp coriander powder

1 tsp red chilli powder

½ tsp garam masala

½ cup oil

Salt to taste

Blend the golden fried onions with the curd in a mixer for a few seconds and keep aside. Heat oil and add garlic, coriander powder, salt, red chilli powder and garam masala powder. Fry the masala for 2 or 3 minutes with half a cup of water. When the oil rises, add the curd and onion mixture. Stir lightly and cook on medium flame for 5 to 8 minutes. When the oil rises, add about 2 cups of water for the gravy. Once it boils, lower the flame and gently add the koftas one by one. Cook on low flame for approximately 25 to 30 minutes. Do not use a ladle and do not cover the lid as the kofta might break. Just move the cooking pot around a bit so the kofta turn and cook evenly. Garnish with fresh coriander.

Note: Ginger paste is not used for the gravy because it breaks the kofta.

Shabdegh

Traditionally, Shabdegh consisted of mutton pieces, kofta and thick chunks of carrot or turnip sliced into halves. These days it is mostly made with just kofta and turnips or carrot. *Shab* in Urdu means night, and the degh would be left to simmer on *dheemi aanch,* low flame, through the night. In earlier days, shabdegh was ordered from professional cooks. Now, many of us make a simpler version at home. Even though it is a winter dish, I am adding this recipe here as a spin-off from the kofta recipe. Kofta are required for shabdegh.

½ kg mincemeat

½ kg thick carrots or turnips

Make the kofta and keep aside. Cut the carrots into 2 to 2 ½" pieces. Slit the thicker pieces lengthwise into two and then scrape out the hard, yellowish part from the upper and middle portion of the carrots. If using turnips, slice them vertically into halves.

Prepare the gravy for the kofta and add carrots or turnips. Once they are half cooked, gently drop the kofta one by one in the gravy. Leave on minimum flame for 25 to 30 minutes till both the kofta and the vegetables are done. Garnish with fresh chopped coriander leaves and a sprinkling of garam masala.

Tamatar Qeema – Tomato Mince

1 kg mincemeat
6–7 medium-sized tomatoes, chopped finely
2 tsp coriander powder
2 tsp garlic paste
1½ tsp ginger paste
5–6 medium-sized onions, golden fried
1 tsp red chilli powder
3–4 green chillies, whole
½ cup oil
Salt to taste

Heat oil and add the fried onions, garlic and ginger paste, coriander powder, red chilli powder and salt. Add a little water and fry the masala for a minute or two. When the oil rises, add the mincemeat. When it is half done, add tomatoes and green chillies. Cook on low flame till the mincemeat is done. Garnish with fresh chopped coriander leaves and a sprinkling of garam masala.

Khadey Masala ka Qeema – Whole Spice Mince

This variety of mincemeat cooked with whole spices is delicious.

1 kg mincemeat
300 gm curd
4 medium-sized onions, sliced
4 black cardamom pods
6–8 cloves
4 tbsp coriander seeds, crushed
6–8 whole red chillies
2–4" cinnamon
8–10 black peppercorns

10-12 pods of garlic, finely chopped
4" ginger, finely chopped
1 medium-sized tomato, chopped
2 bay leaves
½ cup oil
Salt to taste

Heat oil and fry the onions for a few minutes till translucent. Now add whole cloves, cardamoms, peppercorns and cinnamon. After a minute or two, add the mincemeat, ginger, garlic, red chillies and the crushed coriander seeds. Occasionally stir the pot, and cook on high flame till the water from the mincemeat evaporates. When the oil rises, add curd and tomato. Pressure-cook for one whistle or on low flame till the mince is done. Garnish with fresh chopped coriander leaves.

Shaami Kebab

Making shaami kebab can be tricky and requires some practice. Once the mixture is ready, they can be made and frozen. Most of these are now prepared plain but in the old days, Amma would add a *kachumar*, stuffing, in the centre of the kebab. If you plan to freeze the kebab, then do not use onions in the stuffing because they release water and spoil the texture. The best way to ensure good quality meat for shaami kebab is to get the mincemeat made from *pasanda*, boneless chunks from the raan.

Interestingly, shaami kebab have nothing to do with Shaam, the Urdu, Persian and Arabic name for Syria. Why they are called shaami kebab remains a mystery. In Damascus, they have a dish with koftas in gravy – kebab hindi. In much the same way, these have nothing to do with *Hind*, Hindustan.

Kebab Mixture

½ kg mincemeat
1 cup chana dal
1 medium-sized potato
1 medium-sized onion, sliced into four
5-6 whole red chillies
1" ginger

4-5 garlic pods

2 black cardamom pods

4 cloves

1 raw egg

1 tbsp coriander seeds

1 tsp cumin seeds

8-10 peppercorns

Oil for frying

Salt to taste

Stuffing

3-4 onions, finely chopped

Ginger, finely chopped

Green chillies, finely chopped

Mint leaves, finely chopped

1 tsp lemon juice

Salt to taste

Boil the mince with a cup of water along with all the ingredients except the egg. Once the mince is cooked and dry, grind the mixture. Now add the raw egg and mix well. Make small, flat round cakes by rolling them with your palms and put a little stuffing in the centre. Once the kebab are made, leave them in the fridge for a little while so that they set well. Keeping the flame low, shallow fry the kebab lightly on both sides till a golden crust appears. Drain excess oil on a paper towel.

Nargisi Kofta

Nargisi kofta is a rare treat. I am adding this recipe here as these kofta require the prepared shaami kebab mixture. The shaami kebab mixture of half kg mincemeat should be enough to prepare 16 portions of nargisi kofta.

8 hard-boiled eggs
½ kg shaami kebab mixture
16 black peppercorns

Prepare the shaami kebab mixture and divide it into eight equal parts. Flatten each part in your palm and wrap the kebab mixture evenly around the boiled eggs. This coating should not be very thick. Shallow fry the eggs till the kebab layering turns golden brown. Now slice the eggs lengthwise in halves and place a black peppercorn in the middle. The eggs then take the shape of *nargisi aankhien*, beautiful eyes. Add the eggs to the gravy in the serving dish.

Note: Prepare the gravy for nargisi kofta with the recipe for kofta gravy.

Winter

After a gruelling summer and a humid September, which Nani called *sitamgar*, oppressive, Dilliwalas await the pleasant cool months of October and early November. Along with February and March, these months are called *gulabi mausam*, rosy weather. Between October and March is when most weddings and parties take place.

As the temperatures drop, dishes like nihari, paya, shabdegh and haleem that contain more spices are made to keep the body warm. Nihari is traditionally a beef curry that is cooked all night and served at dawn. It is made in a degh that is fixed in a clay enclosure that uses coal or wooden logs for fuel. The degh is sealed while the nihari simmers and is opened early morning. It is said that a little leftover nihari is mixed with the next fresh lot of nihari being prepared. This is called *taar*, believed to be responsible for the unique flavour of the dish. Mamoo Abdullah said that some old shops boasted of an unbroken nihari taar going back to more than a century.

Those days, nihari and shabdegh were ordered from professional cooks and never cooked at home. We ate nihari *nihar muh,* on an empty stomach. Till some years ago, nihari was called *gharibon ka khana,* poor man's food, and considered inappropriate for serving to guests. Over the years, it has come to be treated as a delicacy and is even served at weddings. How things change!

Legend has it that the workers engaged in the construction of Shahjahanabad began their early mornings with nihari that was cooked overnight. This wholesome dish provided them sustenance for the day's hard work. Over the centuries, various herbs, spices and chillies were added to the nihari degh.

At Shama Kothi, in the days when Abba was the head of the family, every winter Sunday was Nihari Day. On Saturday evenings, the drivers carried a large *bartan*, utensil, to the outlet. We were given the first serving of nihari, which is considered the finest. On Sundays, at the crack of dawn, the driver brought the nihari and khamiri roti home. Nihari eateries in the old city still open at dawn and if one is late, you get leftovers.

On Sunday mornings around eight, the whole family was expected to gather for nihari breakfast in the sun-soaked verandah adjoining the garden. The dastarkhwan would be spread out on the floor with all of us sitting on the dari chandni. Plates were warmed in a tub of hot water to prevent the ghee from solidifying. A lighted coal *angheeti*, stove, stood in a corner of the verandah.

As we sat around the dastarkhwan, each one was handed a plateful of nihari with a bhagar of desi ghee and crisp golden fried onions. Plates full of garnish were also laid out. These included chopped ginger, garam masala, sliced green chillies and slices of lemon. Hot khamiri roti, thick round yeast bread baked in a tandoor, accompanied the nihari. These were bought from a well-known rotiwala in the old city.

To neutralize the effect of the hot spices, we finished the meal with a bowlful of *gajarbhatta*, a porridge made from carrots with toppings of malai. We then sat in the sun and ate large *santarey*, oranges, the rarely seen Nagpur variety. This family tradition ended with Abba's death almost thirty-three years ago.

The nihari we had was bought from an eatery near the Tughlaq era Kalan mosque inside Turkman Gate. Since the mosque is commonly called Kali Masjid, this nihari came to be known as 'Kali Masjid ki Nihari'. The small, old style shop with wooden benches continues to do brisk business. Sometimes in winter, Vaseem, my younger brother, and I go there to have nihari at dawn. Although the quality has dropped over the years, it is still worth it. Other popular nihariwalas are Shabrati of Chitli Qabar, Kallu of Daryaganj and Noora of Baada Hindu Rao. Nikki of Baada makes the finest khamiri, baqerkhani and qulcha roti.

In the last many years, cooking nihari at home has become quite popular. Many of my cousins and aunts make it really well. Packaged nihari masalas, especially the ones that come from Pakistan, have made cooking nihari easier. Of course, those who use readymade masala rarely confess to using it! These days I even hear of chicken nihari, which is blasphemous for us Dilliwalas.

Other winter favourites include biryani, qorma, haleem and paya. Haleem is made with mutton, whole wheat and chana dal. Traditionally, it involves a lengthy process of washing, drying the wheat, cooking all the ingredients separately and then deboning the meat, pounding all the ingredients together. I often make haleem with whole-wheat porridge instead of whole wheat grain. However, it does not taste the same as making it with the whole wheat but is almost as good.

Nihari

1 kg mutton shanks

Nihari Masala

3-4 tsp fennel seeds
1 tsp cumin seeds
4 tsp dried ginger powder
1 blade mace
½ nutmeg
4 green cardamoms
4-6 small bay leaves
2" cinnamon
10 cloves
15 black peppercorns
4 black cardamoms

Gravy

2 tsp garlic paste

1 tsp ginger paste

1 tsp red chilli powder

1 tsp deghi red chilli powder

1 cup oil

½ cup whole-wheat flour

Salt to taste

When you purchase mutton, tell the butcher it is for nihari so that he prepares large cuts of adla. I swear by this recipe that Ainee shared with me. She often makes the nihari masala powder and gives it to her family and others who ask for it.

We use both varieties of red chilli powder because while the regular makes it hot and spicy, the deghi adds colour to the dish. If you want the nihari spicier, increase both the chilli powders in equal proportion.

Grind all the ingredients for the masala powder together in the mixer and keep it aside. Heat oil, add garlic and ginger paste, red chilli powder and salt. Fry with a little water for a few minutes till the oil rises. Now add the meat and stir for 5 to 10 minutes till the water it releases evaporates and the oil rises. Then add the powdered nihari masala and continue to stir for a few minutes. Now add 4-5 cups of water. You could pressure-cook for two whistles or leave on low flame till the meat is done.

The wheat flour is used to thicken the nihari and for enhancing taste. Roast the wheat flour over a tawa, or in another utensil for a few minutes. The wheat should turn slightly darker but not brown. Mix the roasted wheat flour with a cup of water, and make sure it does not form lumps. The water and flour mixture is added to the boiling nihari till the right thickness of the gravy is achieved. Leave to simmer for 5 to 10 minutes. The nihari is ready to be served.

However, nihari is best when left for a few hours to mature before serving. I usually take a fistful of golden fried onions and add these to a little piping hot desi ghee and pour it directly on the serving plate so it looks sizzling and inviting. The right garnish for nihari is very important. The traditional way is to keep fresh chopped coriander leaves, finely shredded ginger strips, chopped green chillies and lemons cut into quarters all together in a plate. This allows everyone to choose their garnish.

Gajarbhatta – Carrot Porridge

½ kg carrots, grated

4 cloves

3-4 tbsp desi ghee

½ cup boiled rice (optional)

Sugar to taste

Dilliwalas relish gajarbhatta as a breakfast or pre-breakfast winter dish. The carrot porridge is traditionally had with *baasi*, stale, milk.

The milk sellers were told to keep some leftover milk because matured milk is creamier. In our home, we had gajarbhatta with dollops of malai.

Heat oil and add cloves. After a minute or two, add grated carrots and sugar. Leave on low flame for 15 to 20 minutes and then add boiled rice. Mix it with the carrots and cook for a few more minutes and your carrot porridge is ready. If you add rice, it will not store well and must be consumed within a day or two. Rice is added to soften the texture, but without the rice, it stays well in the fridge for about a week. Gajarbhatta does not take very long to prepare. It is best served with cold milk and fresh cream.

Haleem

1 kg mutton qorma

Mutton qorma is the basic requirement for haleem. Use the recipe for qorma to prepare it. Do not add the kewra and almonds. The meat needs to be cooked till it becomes tender and easy to debone. It is best to use a pressure cooker for two to three whistles, for we need the meat to shed the bone. Allow the meat to cool down.

Debone the meat with your hands. This becomes somewhat messy but it's the only way to ensure complete deboning. You could use boneless meat for haleem. It is simpler and less complicated. I prefer cooking with the bones as the stock adds to the flavour. Keep the deboned qorma aside.

Dal

250 gm chana dal
½ tsp turmeric powder
½ tsp red chilli powder
Salt to taste

This is a simple dal recipe. Boil the dal with about 3 cups of water along with salt, red chilli and turmeric powders. Cook till the dal is soft and ready. Chana dal needs to be soaked in water for a substantial amount of time. Otherwise, you could pressure-cook the dal for two whistles. Keep the ready dal aside.

Wheat

500 gm broken wheat (*chaddi hui*)
½ tsp turmeric
Salt to taste

Soak the wheat overnight in water. Boil it in water with turmeric, salt and cook till soft. The turmeric lends it a little colouring. While boiling, the level of water should be around 3" above the wheat.

Haleem Preparation

Mix the deboned qorma with the prepared wheat and dal. Traditionally, haleem is mashed with a special *ghotni,* wooden ladle. It is like the ladle used to make lassi but without the wedges at the bottom. If you use a mixer, exercise patience. A cup at a time is best and the mixture requires a quick spin. If it is too thick, a little boiled and cooled water can be added while blending. You must make sure that there is no bone left or it will spoil both the haleem and the mixer. I find using an electric hand mixer the best. This enables mixing directly in the utensil.

Haleem must have shreds of meat visible and should not become a thin paste. It is meant to have loch, a gruel-like consistency. The consistency should be just right, not too watery and not too thick. A topping of some sliced golden fried onions added to piping hot desi ghee and poured over the haleem serving perfects the presentation and taste.

Haleem garnishing includes fresh chopped coriander leaves, finely chopped green chillies, garam masala, finely shredded ginger strips and sliced lemon halves. It is eaten with a spoon. I cannot understand how some people eat it with roti for it already contains wheat! Dilliwalas serve haleem with the sweet-sour arq-e-nana chutney, made from raw mangoes, raisins, watermelon, cucumber, lauki and melon seeds. Haleem is a delicacy that has the honour of being a stand-alone dish. When you have haleem, just enjoy haleem.

Paya – Trotters

I often have friends and family over for paya Sunday brunch. There is nothing like trotter soup to keep the body warm. Paya is another stand-alone delicacy.

Sometimes the dish is made with just paya. The only meat cut that is often added to paya is adla. No other meat cut is cooked with paya.

Making paya is rather simple, but one must get the consistency of the soup right. It should not be too watery nor too thick. Ameena Chachi, whom we call Choti Auntie, taught me this recipe many years ago.

Paya requires meticulous cleaning at home, even if the butcher claims to have already done it. The best way to do this is to soak them in warm water for a while. Now, clean them with your hands, making sure that there is no hair left on the bones.

Paya Soup

6 paya
1-2 tsp red chilli powder
2 tsp garlic paste
1 tsp ginger paste
4 tsp coriander powder
½ tsp turmeric powder
Salt to taste

Pressure cookers work well for preparing paya or else they take forever to cook. Boil the paya with about 8-10 cups of water with the red chilli powder, garlic and paste, coriander powder, turmeric powder and salt. Three whistles of the cooker should be enough. If cooking on a low flame, then boil for about an hour. The bones should not break but soften, while the soup must remain slightly thick. It should acquire a *chipchipahat*, stickiness, from the gelatin released by the paya.

Paya Bhagar

3 medium-sized onions, chopped
300 gm curd
1 tsp garam masala
½ cup oil
¼ cup whole-wheat flour (optional)

From the prepared paya, take out the bones and keep aside. In another utensil, heat oil and sauté the onions till they are translucent. Add the curd and garam masala to the onions. Fry till the curd is cooked and then add the paya bones and fry for a few minutes. Now, add the bones and masala to the soup and paya is ready. If you wish to thicken the soup, add a little wheat flour to it. Roast the wheat flour on a flat tava lightly and mix with about half a cup of water, making sure no lumps are formed. Pour this into the boiling paya and leave to simmer for 5 to 10 minutes before turning off the flame.

Paya with Adla – Trotters with Shanks

If cooking paya with shanks, boil the paya as above and keep aside. Cook the shanks separately.

½ kg mutton shanks
3-4 medium-sized onions, golden fried
1 tsp red chilli powder
4 tsp coriander powder
1 tsp garlic paste
¾ tsp ginger paste
200 gm curd (optional)
½-¾ cup oil
Salt to taste

Heat oil, add the garlic, ginger, chilli powder, coriander powder and salt with half a cup of water. Fry the masala for a minute or two. Add shanks and cook on high flame for about 5 to 10 minutes till the water released by the meat evaporates. Once the oil bubbles rise, lower the flame.

Meanwhile blend the golden fried onions and curd together for a few seconds in the mixer and add to shanks. When the curd is cooked and the oil rises, add a cup or two of water, enough to cover the mutton pieces. Pressure-cook for two whistles or leave on low flame till done.

Now mix the shanks with the cooked paya soup and let them simmer together on low flame for about 5 to 10 minutes. If you wish to thicken the consistency of the soup, add a little roasted wheat flour as suggested above. Add some golden fried onions to a little piping hot desi ghee and pour directly over the paya on the serving dish.

Paya garnish includes garam masala, chopped green chillies, fresh chopped coriander leaves, fine strips of ginger and lemon slices. These accompaniments are kept separately, so that each person can add the garnish to their taste. Paya is best served in soup bowls.

Kali Mirch Pasanda – Black Pepper Mutton

Pasanda are flattened boneless pieces of mutton from the raan, leg. The process of flattening requires extra time and effort from the butcher, and they often make a fuss unless you are a regular customer. Bharva pasanda is a popular dish with the Kayastha community of Delhi, but they make it differently from us. As the name suggests, they use a stuffing, we don't. We also cook pasanda with the qorma or basic salan recipe. Paneer pasanda and chicken pasanda recipes are now common, but frankly any pasanda except those made from mutton are a joke!

Kali mirch pasanda is a rather unique specialty of Dilliwalas and are simply awesome. In this version of pasanda, black pepper powder replaces the red chilli powder. A touch of turmeric gives the dish a rich golden hue. If you enjoy pepper steak, I guarantee you will love these pasanda.

1 kg mutton pasanda

5-6 medium-sized onions, golden fried

6 tsp coriander powder

2 tsp black pepper powder, fresh ground

1 tsp garam masala powder

½ tsp turmeric powder

2 tsp ginger paste

1 tsp garlic paste

350-400 gm curd

¾-1 cup oil

Salt to taste

Heat oil and add the black pepper powder, garam masala powder, garlic and ginger paste, turmeric powder, coriander powder and salt. Add a little water and fry the masala for a few minutes till the oil separates from it. Now add the pasanda and stir for 5 to 10 minutes on high flame. When the oil rises, add a cup or two of water and cover the utensil and cook on medium flame.

Meanwhile, blend the golden fried onions and curd in a mixer for a few seconds. Add this mixture to the pasanda when it is half done. Now cook on low flame till the pasanda is tender.

Salan – Mutton with Vegetable

Dilliwalas regularly make salan, that is, adding seasonal vegetables to mutton. There is no concept of *sookhi sabzi*, dry vegetables, in our cuisine. When a dish with mutton and vegetables has gravy, it is called a salan; if not, it becomes gosht – gobi gosht, chuqandar gosht and so on. A large variety of salan are made, each with distinct flavour and taste. The basic method of making various salan is almost the same, except for a slight change in the addition or subtraction of an ingredient or two.

My favourite salan include gajar, matar, shalgam and chuqandar. For health reasons, I don't add too much meat. For everyday cooking, I divide a kilo of meat into two or three packets and freeze them, using one packet at a time. This way, one gets the flavour of salan, while eating more vegetables.

Basic Salan Recipe

½ kg mutton

4-5 medium-sized onions, golden fried

1 tsp garlic paste

¾ tsp ginger paste

1 tsp red chilli powder

3-4 tbsp coriander powder

200 gm curd, lightly beaten

½ tsp turmeric

½ cup oil

Salt to taste

Heat oil and add the fried onions, garlic, ginger, chilli powder, coriander powder and salt with half a cup of water, so that the masala does not burn. Fry the masala for 2 to 3 minutes till the oil separates from it. Add the meat, stir occasionally and cook on high flame for about 5 to 10 minutes so that the water released by the meat evaporates and oil bubbles rise.

Now lower the flame and add about two cups of water. As a rule, the level of water should remain a few inches above the meat. If making a salan, the quantity of water is generally more than when making a gosht. This depends on the vegetable being cooked with the mutton. When making salan with a vegetable that release a lot of water, less water is used.

Cover the utensil and leave the mutton on medium flame till half done. If using the pressure cooker, allow for one whistle. Add the vegetable and leave covered on low flame till both the vegetable and mutton are nearly done. Now add the beaten curd and leave to simmer for another 10 minutes till both the vegetable and mutton are done.

With some practice, you will figure out at what stage different vegetables should be added to the meat. Vegetables such as potatoes, peas, carrots and turnips require more time and are added when the meat is half done. Lighter greens are added when the meat is nearly done as they take less time to cook.

Note: In a slight variation of the traditional salan recipe given above, I usually add the curd after frying the meat. Stirring occasionally, I let it cook for about 5-8 minutes. Then I add water and pressure-cook the mutton for one whistle before adding the vegetable. This gives the dish a richer deghi texture. You can make salan with either of the two methods.

Shola

Shola is traditionally made with leftover qorma with dal, spinach and rice added to it. It is a unique dish associated with our community.

½ kg mutton
500-600 gm spinach, finely chopped (palak)
125 gm rice, preferably broken basmati (unsoaked)
125 gm split green moong dal (chilkey wali)

Prepare the meat base with the basic salan recipe. Add the curd to the meat and cook it before adding the spinach. Let the meat cook in the water released by the spinach. Pressure-cook for one whistle or leave on medium flame till the meat is half done. Now add rice and dal along with about 3 cups of water, the level being about 2-3" above the rice. Leave on low flame and cook till all the ingredients are done. Use a wooden ladle to mash the mixture lightly.

Top the dish with a dollop of desi ghee and golden fried onions. Garnish includes finely sliced ginger strips, chopped green chilles and lemon slices. These are kept on a separate plate along with the shola dish.

Sem Beej Salan – Green Fava Beans with Mutton

½ kg green fava beans

½ kg mutton

1 tsp dried methi

Sem ke beej are a favourite with Dilliwalas. Unfortunately, these beans are not easily available. They are sold in Maliwara, Ballimaran and Phatak Habash Khan mohallas. I make an effort to cook sem ke beej at least once in winter for old times' sake.

Soak the fava beans in warm saline water for about 15 to 20 minutes. Then, peel away the outer layer. It's a bit tedious, but worth the effort. Sem ke beej are cooked with the basic salan recipe. Add the beans to the meat when it is half done as they take a while to cook. Just before turning off the flame, add a spoon of dry methi leaves for enhancing the taste.

Matar Salan – Peas with Mutton

Sometimes Dilliwalas make aloo matar salan, by adding both peas and potatoes to the meat. I do this often and it creates an enjoyable, wholesome meal. I recommend that you try this combination.

½ kg shelled green peas

½ kg mutton

Prepare matar salan with the basic salan recipe. Sometimes I blend one or two medium-sized tomatoes along with the curd. Add the peas to the mutton when it is half done. If using a pressure cooker, it would require one whistle for the meat and another after adding the peas. Garnish with fresh chopped coriander leaves.

Boont Salan – Green Chickpeas with Mutton

½ kg mutton
½ kg fresh green chickpeas

Boont are available during the cold months and disappear by March or early April. As children, we roasted whole shrubs of it on a bonfire. They crackled in the fire and tasted warm and wonderful. To make boont salan, use the basic salan recipe. Add the boont to the meat when it is half done.

Gajar Salan – Carrots with Mutton

½ kg carrots
½ kg mutton

Several friends have tasted gajar salan in my home for the first time. Some are surprised at the combination of carrots and meat. I tell them that we eat almost all vegetables with meat! You must try gajar salan to believe how sumptuous it is. It's an exciting way to eat carrots, which are so nutritious.

Gajar salan is made with the basic salan recipe. Simply add two medium-sized tomatoes along with the curd to reduce the sweetness of the carrot. Ideally, carrots for this recipe should be thick and large, sliced into 2" pieces. Slit the thicker pieces lengthwise into two and then scrape out the hard, yellowish part from the upper and middle portion of the carrots. Add the carrots when the meat is half done. Garnish with fresh chopped coriander leaves.

Shalgam Salan – Turnips with Mutton

½ kg turnips
½ kg mutton

Shalgam salan is made with the basic salan recipe. Cut the turnips vertically into halves and add to the meat when it is half done. If using the pressure cooker, it's one whistle for the meat and another after adding the shalgam. Garnish with fresh chopped coriander leaves and a sprinkling of garam masala.

Nashpati Salan – Pears with Mutton

½ kg cooking pears
½ kg mutton

Nashpati salan requires cooking pears that are a little hard. Peel and slice the pears into halves and remove the seed part in the centre. Nashpati salan is prepared with the basic salan recipe. Add the pears to the meat when it is half done. Garnish with fresh chopped coriander leaves.

Kela Salan – Bananas with Mutton

6–8 raw bananas
½ kg mutton

We had a banana tree at home, so Amma plucked raw bananas and cooked them with meat. Once a a popular dish with Dilliwalas, few make it these days. I had not eaten it for decades until I recently tried it before including the recipe in this book. It is delicious and can be made at any time of the year.

Prepare kela salan with the basic salan recipe. Cut the bananas into small one inch rounds and fry lightly. Add the bananas to the meat when it is almost done. You can use the pressure cooker for the meat, but not after adding the bananas. Garnish with fresh chopped coriander leaves.

Gobi Gosht – Cauliflower with Mutton

1 kg cauliflower

½ kg mutton

2-3 tbsp shredded ginger

Prepare gobi gosht with the basic salan recipe. Add the cauliflower to the meat when it is half done, along with finely sliced ginger strips. Leave on low flame till the meat and cauliflower are both done. The cauliflower is used in a larger quantity because it reduces during cooking.

Gobi gosht is *bhuna*, not watery, so if there is water left, then dry the excess water. As cauliflower is said to be *baadi*, not easily digestible, it requires a garnish of shredded ginger strips and plenty of fresh chopped corainder leaves.

Chuqandar Gosht – Beetroot with Mutton

1 kg beetroot

250-300 gm spinach

½ kg mutton

Beetroot and meat is another unusual combination that Dilliwalas relish. Beetroots are sweet, so some spinach or beetroot leaves are added to the dish. When I made a fuss as a child, Apa Saeeda almost force-fed me saying, '*Chuqandar se khoon banta hai*,' beetroots increase your blood count! I grew to love them as she made them so well.

There are two way of cutting beetroot. Amma would slice them in half, then cut them into wafer-thin slices. Apa Saeeda grated the beetroot, and since I learnt from her, I do the same. I prefer the shredded beets but this is a personal choice.

Since beetroots melts and reduce while cooking, it is best to use 1 kg for ½ kg mutton. Make chuqandar gosht with the basic

salan recipe. Add the beetroot to the meat when it is half done. To reduce the sweetness, add a small bunch of palak leaves weighing 250-300 gram.

Sometimes, I make it without the spinach and still love the taste. This dish is not meant to be watery, so if there is water left in the cooking utensil, cook on high flame and dry the excess water. A fresh green chutney made of garlic, green chillies and coriander leaves is mixed with chuqandar gosht after the cooking is done. It adds a tangy taste.

Green chutney for Chuqandar Gosht

A few pods of garlic
Few green chillies
Small bunch of fresh coriander leaves
Small bunch of fresh mint leaves
½ tsp dried raw mango powder (amchoor)
Salt to taste

Grind all the above ingredients in a mixer and the chutney is ready.

Gandley Gosht – Mustard Greens with Mutton

1½ kg shredded gandley (sarson saag)
½ kg shredded spinach (palak)
½ kg mutton
3–4 tbsp shredded ginger

Sarson saag, that is mustard greens, is made with and without meat. Dilliwalas prefer sarson with mutton, we call it gandley gosht. The leaves and the stems close to the leaves should be washed thoroughly and finely chopped.

Prepare the meat with the basic salan recipe. Don't use too much water while cooking the meat base as spinach will release a lot of water. When the meat is half done, add sarson and palak along with shredded ginger strips. Leave on low flame till done. This is not a gravy dish, so make sure that the excess water has dried. Garnish with shredded ginger strips.

Dal Gosht – Lentil with Mutton

300 gm kg chana dal
½ kg mutton qorma or plain salan

Dal

300 gm chana dal
½ tsp turmeric powder
1 level tsp red chilli powder
½ tsp garlic paste
Salt to taste

Prepare dal gosht with the basic salan recipe and make sure that the meat is done. Then, remove the oil layer and set aside. If it is left in the utensil, the chana dal will later absorb it all up.

Ideally chana dal should be soaked in water for a few hours before cooking. Boil the dal with turmeric, red chilli, garlic paste and salt. Add just enough water for the dal to cook while remaining whole. If using a pressure cooker, one whistle is enough. When the dal is ready, add to the mutton qorma. Take the oil set aside and pour over the serving dish. Garnish with *sookha pudina*, dried mint, or fresh mint leaves and a sprinkling of garam masala.

Lobia Gosht – Black Eyed Peas with Mutton

1 kg black eyed peas
½ kg mutton
2-3 tbsp shredded ginger strips

Prepare lobia gosht with the basic salan recipe. Destring the lobia and cut them into half inch pieces. Add the sliced lobia to the meat when it is half done along with the shredded ginger strips. Garnish with shredded ginger strips.

Matar Qeema – Green Pea Mince

½ kg shelled green peas

½ kg mincemeat

4 medium-sized tomatoes, chopped

1 tsp red chilli powder

2 whole green chillies

1 tsp coriander powder

1 tsp garlic paste

¾ tsp ginger paste

3-4 medium-sized onions

2-3 tbsp shredded ginger strips

Salt to taste

Heat oil and fry the onions to golden brown. Now add garlic, ginger, coriander powder, chilli powder and salt. Fry for a few minutes, then add the mincemeat. When it is half done, add tomatoes and stir for 5 to 10 minutes before leaving on low flame. It is better to skin the tomatoes, but this is not necessary. Add peas, ginger strips and whole green chillies to the mincemeat when it is half done. Leave on low flame till the mincemeat and peas are tender.

Traditionally, matar qeema is cooked with curd instead of tomatoes. I prefer using tomatoes. They add both taste and colour to the dish. You could replace the tomatoes with 200 gm curd. Garnish with fresh chopped coriander leaves and a sprinkling of garam masala.

Kachri Qeema – Marinated Smoked Mince

Kachri is a small, wild brown melon found in desert areas. It is a common ingredient in Rajasthani cuisine. We use it as a food tenderizer and it is available at spice stores in both whole and

powder form. Kachri spoil easily on contact with moisture and should be stored in airtight containers. Whole kachri stay better and it is best to crush them when needed.

Kachri qeema is a specialty and not many outside our community know of this dish. It is amongst my son Arman's favourite dishes. He claims it transports him straight to paradise! Each time I make it, he begins inviting his friends over and it doesn't last very long on the table. This is an absolute must-try recipe.

Marination

1 kg mincemeat
4 whole kachris crushed or 2 tsp kachri powder
1 cup half-ripe papaya, peeled and pulped
1–1½ tsp red chilli powder
1 tsp garam masala
2 tsp garlic paste
1 tsp ginger paste
Salt to taste

Marinate the mincemeat with all the above ingredients. Leave overnight in the fridge or at least for four to five hours.

Cooking the Mincemeat

300 gm curd
4 medium-sized onions, golden fried
4 cloves
4 green cardamoms (optional)
½ cup oil

Mix the curd and onions with the marinated mincemeat an hour before cooking. Heat oil and add the cloves and cardamoms and leave for a minute or two till they crackle. Now add the marinated mincemeat. Stir for a few minutes on medium flame and then leave on low flame till done. Do not use the pressure cooker. This is a dry dish, so let the water released from the mincemeat evaporate fully.

After the mincemeat is cooked, prepare to smoke it. Light a small piece of coal over the stove flame, then place it on an onion slice, pour a few drops of oil on the live coal so it smokes. Then, leave the smoking coal over the qeema and cover the cooking pot with a lid. Let it remain there for a few minutes. I sometimes use a long deep spoon, place the smoking coal on it and close the lid. It adds an exceptional smoked aroma.

Garnish with fresh chopped coriander leaves, onion rings, chopped green chillies, shredded ginger strips and a sprinkling of garam masala. A squeeze of lemon juice adds a bit of tanginess.

Palak Qeema – Spinach Mince

1 kg spinach
½ kg mincemeat
150 gm methi (optional)

Palak qeema is made with the same recipe as the matar qeema. Replace the tomatoes with 200 to 250 gm curd. In palak qeema, a fistful of fresh chopped methi leaves or a teaspoon of dried methi leaves is usually added along with the palak to enhance the flavour.

Lobia Qeema – Black Eyed Peas Mince

½ kg lobia
½ kg mincemeat
2-3 whole green chillies

Lobia salan and lobia qeema are both specialties of Dilliwalas. For lobia qeema, use the matar qeema recipe, replacing the peas with lobia beans. Also, make sure to replace the tomatoes with 200 gm of curd. Destring the lobia and then cut in fine pieces. Add the green chillies and lobia to the mince when it is half done. Garnish with shredded ginger strips.

Murgh Musallam – Whole Chicken

Murgh musallam was once a favoured dish in Emperor Akbar's court. It was part of the staple banquet cuisine in Delhi. Khala Rabia, Ammi's older sister makes the best murgh musallam in the family. Khala lives in the Kishanganj Mohalla near Hindu Baada Rao. I enjoy visiting her house, which has a traditional courtyard and large sunken mirrors on the wall with borders of rare English floral tiles. This is Khala's recipe.

1 kg whole chicken

Marination

3 tsp cumin seeds, roasted
8 black peppercorns
2 lemons
2 medium-sized onions, chopped
2 tsp ginger paste
2 tsp garlic paste
1-1½ tsp red chilli powder
250-300 gm curd
Salt to taste

Stuffing

2 medium-sized onions, finely chopped
2 eggs, hard boiled
Saffron or saffron colouring

4-5 green chillies, finely chopped

Roasted almonds (optional)

Roasted cashew nuts (optional)

Cooking

6 cloves

6 green cardamoms

½ cup oil

Wash the chicken well and prick all around with a fork. Then make a few cuts so the marinating mixture goes deep inside. Grind all the spices together in a mixer and add the lemon juice. Marinate the chicken all over with this paste. Leave for a few hours in the fridge.

Dip the boiled eggs in a few strands of saffron or a little saffron colouring soaked in a tablespoon of milk, otherwise the eggs will remain a bland white. Place these peeled, hard-boiled eggs and the rest of the stuffing inside the stomach hollow. Khala Rabia stitches the chicken up with a needle and thread. I tie a thick cotton thread and crisscross it to seal the stuffing and keep the chicken whole.

Once the chicken is sewn tightly, heat oil, add cloves and cardamoms. Crackle them for a minute or two and then place the chicken in the utensil. Use a wide pan that takes the whole chicken comfortably. Toss it around gently so it colours evenly and then leave for about half-an-hour on low flame till ready. Serve whole on a large rice dish and pour the leftover gravy over it. If you wish to dress the dish extravagantly, make a ring of dry fruits such as raisins, roasted cashews, almonds and pine nuts around the murgh musallam. Carve on the dining table.

A food stall near Jama Masjid, Delhi

Fish

Dilliwalas love fish, but have rules regarding their consumption. They mostly eat fish in the months that contain the letter 'r'. We begin cooking in September and continue till April. I don't know exactly when and how these informal rules came to be established. One obvious reason appears to be that because fish has garam taseer, it is best enjoyed in winter. The other reason is that since Dilliwalas traditionally got their fish from the Yamuna river, they did not fish during breeding season.

Before the advent of refrigerated transport facilities, Dilliwalas were dependent on the fresh catch from the Yamuna. Now Delhi gets fish from Gujrat, Mumbai and other parts of the country. Earlier we got fish from the fish market near Jama Masjid, but now it is easier for me to buy from markets in New Delhi.

Dilliwalas mostly relish fish either in a salan or fried. Fish tikka are a recent addition. Food stalls near the Jama Masjid have been known for the best fried fish. I maintain the family tradition of going there occasionally to enjoy their fried fish during winter.

Machli Salan – Fish Curry

The preferred variety of fish for is singhara, a river fish with a central bone. Fish sellers know how make different cuts for frying, baking and curry dishes. You can have it deboned, but it just doesn't taste the same, for bone stock adds flavour to the dish.

1 kg fish, sliced
6-7 medium-sized onions, golden fried
2 tsp garlic paste
1 tsp ginger paste
1½-2 tsp red chilli powder

6 tbsp coriander powder

6 cloves

6-8 green cardamom pods

400 gm curd

½ cup oil

1 tsp dried methi leaves (optional)

Salt to taste

Blend the fried onions with the curd and keep the mixture aside. Heat oil and add cloves and green cardamoms. After a minute or two, add garlic and ginger paste, coriander powder, salt and red chilli powder. Remember to add a little water so that the masala does not burn. After a few minutes, when oil bubbles surface, add the onion and curd mixture. Cook for 5 to 10 minutes till the bubbles rise. Lastly, add the fish pieces and cook for 10 to 15 minutes on low flame till done. Add dried methi to the fish a few minutes before turning off the flame. Keep a check on the fish so that the pieces don't break with excess cooking. Garnish with a sprinkling of garam masala.

Machli Salan is best enjoyed with basmati rice. I like to heat a little desi ghee and add a teaspoon of cumin seeds and a little salt before adding the rice and leaving it to cook.

Tali Machli – Fish Fry

Although Dilliwalas prefer singhada for frying, this recipe can be used for other varieties of fish.

1 kg fish, sliced

2 tsp garlic paste

1 tsp ginger paste

2-3 tsp red chilli powder

2 tsp garam masala

250 gm curd, thick
½ tsp turmeric
Gram flour (besan) for coating
Salt to taste

Marinate the fish with all the above ingredients for 4 to 6 hours. Then coat the pieces of fish with gram flour and deep fry in piping hot oil. The flour can be dry or made into thick batter by adding a little water and a pinch of salt. Spread the fried fish on paper towels to soak the excess oil. Serve with fresh green or any other chutney.

Matar ki Phaliyaan – Peas in the Pod

½ kg peas in the pod
½ tsp red chilli powder
2-3 tbsp tamarind water
Salt to taste

Matar ki Phaliyan remind me of my childhood when we had these as evening snacks on the arrival of winter. The peas must be from the first fresh crop of the season that are both soft and sweet.

Wash the whole peas with the *chilka*, outer covering, thoroughly. Boil these in half a cup of water with red chilli powder and salt. Keep on low flame or, if using the pressure cooker, let it cook for one whistle. Meanwhile, mix some tamarind in a little water. Run this water through a sieve and pour over the cooked whole peas. Serve these peas in the pod on a platter.

The proper method of eating matar ki phaliyan is *daant se soonthna*, to slide and scrape them with the teeth. This way one gets the combined taste of the pulp from the pod and the peas.

Shalgam Bhujia – Turnip Crush

Dilliwalas relish shalgam in any form. Cooking turnips with meat or without are both popular in winter. Shalgam Bhujia is easy and quick to prepare. Apa Saeeda taught me this recipe.

1 kg turnips
10–12 garlic pods
2 tsp cumin seeds
5-6 red chillies, whole
150–200 gm curd
¼ cup oil
Salt to taste

Boil the turnips with the skin. Turnips are best boiled in a pressure cooker with one whistle. Once done, peel and mash the turnips. You can use a fork or the special ladle used for mashing potatoes.

Chop the garlic into small rounds. Heat oil and add the garlic. When it turns light brown, add cumin seeds and leave for a minute till they crackle. Now add chopped red chillies and salt. Then add the mashed turnips and fry for a few minutes before adding the lightly beaten curd. Stir occasionally and leave on low flame for 5 to 10 minutes. Garnish with fresh chopped coriander leaves.

Bathua Roti – Spinach Roti

Bathua is a saag available only in winter. Dilliwalas make rotis with this variety of spinach. Bathua Roti with plain curd and a little pickle on the side is by itself a wholesome meal. This was one of Apa Saeeda's regular treats for us during winter. She taught me this recipe. Once the bathua roti mixture is ready, it can be stored it in the fridge for a few days and pulled out to make fresh roti when required.

½ kg whole-wheat flour
1 kg bathua

1 tsp carom seeds (ajwain)

1 tsp cumin seeds

1 tsp garlic paste

Salt to taste

Pluck the bathua leaves and clean them thoroughly. Then boil them for around 10 minutes and strain. Now, add to regular whole-wheat flour and mix the two well. The wheat will take on a green colour. Add the remaining ingredients to the dough.

Make roti on a regular tava. Use oil, or preferably a little desi ghee, to spread over the tava before making the roti. When cooking the roti on the flip side, oil the tava again. Place the roti on a paper towel to drain excess oil. This is best served with fresh curd and pickle.

Winter Sweet Dishes

Winter sweets such as panjiri and satora are made with *gond*, edible gum crystal, semolina and dry fruits. These are mixed and made into small round balls, stored in jars and had in small portions. They help in keeping the body warm. Satora does not have *gond* and is softer. It is spread on large round trays, and cut in *lauzaat,* diamond shapes. Amma and Apa Saeeda made these but unfortunately I do not have recipes for them.

Maleeda

I associate maleeda with my childhood as Apa Saeeda made it for us in winter. She said the bajra, pearl millet, and *gur,* jaggery, would keep us warm. Gur is also beneficial for health. Apa Saeeda would bring fresh jaggery from her home in Baghpat. We loved maleeda and ate it as dessert. I often make it during winter for my family as it is not quite the dish to serve guests!

½ kg bajra flour

½ kg jaggery

6-8 tbsp desi ghee

Make regular roti using bajra flour, which is easily available. Sometimes, I send for fresh bajra flour from stores that have a *chakki*, flour-making apparatus. This is one way of ensuring that the flour is not stale.

Break the roti into one half inch or smaller pieces and add some desi ghee. Break the jaggery into tiny pieces as well. You could grate the jaggery, but I prefer it hand crushed. Mix the jaggery well with the roti and your maleeda is ready.

Anday ka Halwa – Egg Halwa

6-8 egg yolks

1½-2 litre milk

4 green cardamoms

3-4 tbsp desi ghee

Few strands of saffron

½ cup sugar or to taste

Anday ka Halwa is traditionally made with *desi andey*, farm eggs. Since these are not easily available, you could prepare it with regular eggs. At home, we use both the egg white and yolks and it tastes equally good. However, if you choose to cook it in the old authentic style, just use the egg yolks.

Heat ghee and add the crushed cardamoms and let them crackle for a minute. Beat the egg yolks along with the milk and sugar and add to the ghee. Adding a few strands of saffron will give it an exquisite flavour. If you don't have saffron, use a pinch of saffron colouring. Cook on low flame till the oil separates from the halwa. Remember, keep stirring so that the milk does not curdle.

A view of the goolar tree from my balcony

Summer

As the leaves of the amaltas and gulmohar trees change their hues to yellow and orange, the heat intensifies in Delhi. Dry heat has never bothered the Dilliwalas as much as the humidity that follows during and after the monsoon months. I grew up hearing that *Dilli ki loo*, the hot dry Delhi wind, is healthy. Nani Amma said that the intense heat killed the unhealthy germs in the body. When the rains arrive, all kinds of viruses pollute the humid air.

Dilliwalas have quaint methods to prevent the intense heat from affecting them and of keeping hydrated. Abba would keep an onion in his kurta pocket to prevent heatstroke. If one of us suffered a heatstroke, onions were placed in the armpits. Fever resulting from excess heat was treated by boiling raw mango slices in water and sprinkling it all over the body.

Since Shama Kothi had long open corridors, large curtains made of khus reed covered the open areas. Spraying these with water transformed the harsh hot wind into a fragrant cool breeze. Even though we had refrigerators, we drank water from a *surahi*, earthen pitcher. A tin-plated copper *katora*, bowl, would be placed upside down over the surahi. Amma said that drinking water from a copper bowl had health benefits.

The change of season brought sparkling colours and scents to our home. The aroma of sandal, unaab, bazuri, gauzaban, falsa, bel and charon maghaz sharbet being made filled the air. These thirst quenchers were served mixed with a spoonful of *tukhme rehan,* tulsi seeds, to enhance their cooling effect. Amma boiled large quantities of barley, mixed it with the sharbet for us to drink through the day. Barley is said to have a cooling effect on the body.

Amma had planted a *bel*, wood-apple tree, near the entrance gate. She never lived to enjoy its fruit. When planting the sapling, she told Ammi that her grandchildren would benefit from the tree. We did, and enjoyed bel sharbet summer after summer. Fresh bel sharbet is such a wonderful, healthy treat in summer

Gonni, khirni, shahtoot and kaseru are some summer fruits which are now not easily available. When feeling nostalgic, I sometimes go to Maliwara and Ballimaran where one can find these.

I remember many kachnar trees around Diplomatic Enclave, near Shama Kothi. Apa Saeeda took us for evening walks where we gathered clusters of kachnar flowers that were strewn on street pavements. Apa Saeeda made delightful sabzi from these pink and white flowers.

Cooking sangri with mutton is probably exclusive to our community. Amma would send the gardener to pluck the fruit. Sangri trees are of moderate size and flower in March, its fruit are the shape of slender, long, cylindrical pods. Sangri trees can be sighted in Lodhi Gardens, some parts of Chanakyapuri and a few other areas where Delhi's original flora still exist. Once abundant in the city, it is now listed amongst Delhi's endangered trees.

The other day, while on a recipe-collecting trip to Choti Auntie's, home in Civil Lines, I was served sangri salan. I asked her where she managed to get the sangri from, since I hadn't seen eaten it in decades. It is available in a few mohlallas of the old city, where many families from our community live. She had it purchased from Haveli Hissamuddin Haider in Ballimaran. It must be bought from the vendors at dawn. If you are late, the sangri is sold out. Sangri is available in May for a short period of fifteen days and for ₹600 a kilo. But whatever the cost and the difficulty in acquiring sangri, Dilliwalas enjoy sangri salan at least once in summer. With Auntie's recipe, I have begun to make sangri at home.

Goolar is another fruit cooked in our homes. Also a local Delhi tree, goolar are like small figs, distinctly arranged in clusters that grow on the tree trunk and main branches. Goolar trees fruit twice a year, once around mid April, and the second, just before the Delhi monsoon disappears.

Luckily, there is a goolar tree in the park right across my flat in Nizamuddin East. A tall tree, its branches almost touch the balcony. Although I have lived here for over ten years, making goolar sabzi never occurred to me. Not having eaten it in decades, I had forgotten its taste. While I was writing this book, Choti Auntie gave me the recipe and I resolved to try it.

I had my eyes on the growing clusters and had thought of getting Sabir to climb the tree. But before I could put this plan in action, I saw a young lad climb the tree and pluck all the fruit. He informed me that his Begum Sahiba had asked him to pick the goolar. He worked for Bushra, my neighbour, who belongs to the same community as me.

I requested that he ask Begum Sahiba to send some of the goolar sabzi for us. The delicious meal arrived just in time for dinner and has since become my son's favourite vegetarian dish. Bushra continues to send me the sabzi frequently. This recipe comes from her. Now we split the goolar and I have begun to cook it regularly.

Goolar trees must be guarded in the season of Eid al Azha, as shepherd boys move around the colony looking to cut down the leaves, a favoured feed for goats. I usually allow these youngsters to prune the tree and take of a few small branches. Once, when I was out of town before the festive season, much to my horror, the tree was stripped of almost all its branches.

Kachnar Kali Salan – Flower Buds with Mutton

The Latin name for kachnar trees is *Bauhinia Variegata*. These trees are of two varieties. The flowers of one are pure white and the other are deep pink in colour. It is a medium-sized tree that can be seen on Delhi's streets and in gardens. Kachnar is said to have many medicinal properties.

Kachnar flowers can be gathered from trees or bought in some vegetable markets of the old city. I buy them from the Punjabi Phatak in Ballimaran where many of the Saudagaran community reside. They are available for about two weeks from the middle of March. One can prepare a vegetable with just the petals or use the whole flower. Kachnar buds are cooked with meat.

½ kg kachnar buds
½ kg meat
100 gm shelled green peas (optional)

Boil the buds in plain water for 2 to 3 minutes. Strain and keep aside. Prepare the meat base with the basic salan recipe. Add the kachnar buds and peas to the meat when it is half done. Leave to cook on low flame till done. A handful of green peas are usually cooked with kachnar buds to reduce its *kasail*, slight bitter taste.

Photo: Arman Ali Dehlvi

Kachnar Bharta – Kachnar Crush

½ kg kachnar flowers
4-5 medium-sized onions, chopped
½ tsp red chilli powder
¼ cup oil
300 gm curd, lightly beaten
¼ tsp turmeric
Salt to taste

Wash and boil the flowers in some water for 2 or 3 minutes and drain. Now blend the flowers in the mixer for a few seconds. Heat oil and fry the onions till translucent. Then add chilli powder, turmeric and salt. Fry for a few minutes till the oil separates. Now add the blended flowers and cook for about another 10 minutes and then add curd. Leave on low flame for 10 to 15 minutes till oil bubbles rise and your flower dish is ready.

Goolar Bharta – Goolar Crush

½ kg goolar
300–350 gm curd
1 tsp red chilli powder
1 tbsp corainder powder
¼ tsp turmeric
¼ tsp raw green mango powder (amchoor)
¼ cup oil
Salt to taste

The goolar should be green, the overripe brownish ones are not for cooking.

Wash the goolar thoroughly and slice off the small stem portion. Boil them in a little water till they turn soft. You may also pressure-cook the goolar for one whistle. Now grind the goolar with the curd in a mixer into a thick paste. Heat oil and fry the onions till translucent and then add chilli powder, coriander powder, turmeric and salt. Fry for a minute or two before adding the goolar and curd mixture. Stir occasionally and leave on low flame for 10 to 15 minutes till oil bubbles rise. Just before turning off the flame, add the dried raw mango powder.

Khatti Meethi Aam Chutney – Sweet and Sour Mango Chutney

1 green raw mango
¼ tsp red chilli powder
1 tsp sugar
Salt to taste

Boil the raw mango and separate the pulp. Now add the sugar, chilli powder and salt to the pulp. The chutney stays well in the fridge for a few days. The amount of sugar or chillies can be adjusted to taste.

Bhindi Salan – Okra with Mutton

½ kg okra
½ kg mutton

Prepare bhindi salan with the regular salan recipe. Make sure you buy small or medium-sized okra. The large ones are generally not used for salan. Cut the stem but be careful not to slice through the main part or else it will leave *lace*, sticky residue. Cook the meat till three-fourth done because okra take little time to cook. Now, add okra and two whole green chillies and cook on slow flame for 10 to 15 minutes till done. Don't pressure the okra or it will break. Garnish with fresh chopped coriander leaves.

Sangri Salan – Sangri with Mutton

1 kg sangri
½ kg mutton
Salt to taste

Wash and cut the sangri into 1" pieces. Boil the sangri in water for 3 to 5 minutes. Drain the water and keep the sangri aside. Prepare the meat base with the basic salan recipe. The quantity of curd, oil and other spices should be slightly increased as sangri requires more masala. Add the sangri to the meat when it is nearly done and leave on low flame for 10 to 15 minutes.

Nun Paani Achaar

Sangri salan is always accompanied by a fresh raw mango, salt and garlic chutney made in water. It is called nun paani ka achaar. Nun, the Urdu alphabet for 'n', stands for namak. Make a small quantity of it, for it is usually had with just this one dish. It requires no oil and stays for a few days.

1 raw green mango, peeled and cut into ½" pieces

¼ tsp chilli powder

¼ tsp Nigella seeds (kalonji)

½ tsp fennel seeds (saunf)

4-6 small garlic pods, whole

A pinch of turmeric

Mix with all other ingredients in half a cup of water and bring to a boil. Then lower the flame and leave to simmer for about 10-15 minutes till the mango is cooked.

Tindey Salan – Round Gourd with Mutton

½ kg mutton

½ kg round gourd

Tindey salan is regular summer fare. Prepare it with the basic salan recipe. Slice the tinda into two halves and add to the meat when it is half done. Garnish with fresh coriander leaves.

Ghiya Gosht – Bottle Gourd with Mutton

1 kg bottle gourd

½ kg of mutton

Ghiya is also commonly called lauki. Slice the ghiya in oblong 1" pieces. Prepare ghiya gosht with the basic salan recipe. Ghiya is added to the meat when it is half done. Ghiya releases a lot of water, which is why one uses double the weight of the meat. Garnishing with dried mint leaves is a must. If you don't have dried mint, then use fresh mint leaves. Ghiya gosht is best served with *khushka*, plain boiled rice.

Arvi Salan – Colocasia Root with Mutton

½ kg colocasia root

½ kg mutton

Prepare arvi salan with the basic salan recipe. Peel the arvis and keep them whole. It is important to remember that arvi is hard and needs more time to cook. Add arvi to the meat when it is slightly less than half done. You could pressure-cook for one or two whistles. Arvi salan is garnished with fresh chopped coriander leaves and served with a kachumar, that is a mixture of chopped onions, lemon juice and chopped green chillies.

Turiayan Gosht – Ridge Gourd with Mutton

1½ kg ridge gourd

½ kg mutton

1 small raw green mango, peeled, grated or finely chopped

2 medium-sized onions, finely sliced

Turaiyan is also called tori. Prepare the meat base with the basic salan recipe without using the curd. In turaiyan gosht, the vegetable is added before the meat is half done. This is to allow the meat to cook in the water released by the turaiyan. Unlike most salan, no extra water is required.

Cut the turaiyan into small rounds. After adding the meat to the masala, cook it for about 10 minutes till the oil rises. Now, add the raw green mango and raw onions along with turaiyan to the meat. Leave on low flame till done. You can also pressure-cook for one whistle and then leave on low flame. This is not a watery dish, so dry excess water. Garnish with dried or fresh mint leaves.

Bhuni Moong Dal – Dry Yellow Lentil

250 kg moong dal

½ tsp red chilli powder

1 tsp garlic paste

½ tsp ginger paste

1 tsp cumin seeds

2 cloves

2 black cardamoms

1" cinnamon

4-6 peppercorns

2 bay leaves

¼ tsp turmeric powder

¼ cup oil

Salt to taste

Soak the dal for half-an-hour and no more. Heat oil and add all the spices and fry for a minute or two. And the dal and fry for a few more minutes. Add a cup of water and leave on low flame till the dal is cooked. The dal must not be watery or squashed and should remain whole. Garnish with chopped coriander, finely cut green chillies, shredded ginger strips and lemon slices.

Karela Qeema – Bitter Gourd Mince

Karela qeema is my favourite qeema and I make it all through the summer months, when karela and raw mangoes are in plenty. I find most people, other than Dilliwalas, don't know about this dish. Most friends try it for the first time in my home and seem to love it. I now get requests for karela qeema all the time.

½ kg bitter gourd
½ kg mincemeat
2-3 medium-sized onions, golden fried
2-3 medium-sized raw onions, finely sliced
1 medium-sized raw green mango, peeled and grated
1 tsp red chilli powder
1 tsp garlic paste
¾ tsp ginger paste
½ tsp turmeric powder
2 green chillies, whole

2 tsp coriander powder

½ cup oil

Salt to taste

Scrape the karela with a knife till the dark green uneven skin comes off. Then place them in a bowl of water with a tsp of salt. Leave for at least half-an-hour. This helps remove the bitterness from the karela. Now slice the karela into half inch rings. Don't throw the seeds. Fry karela rings along with seeds to a light golden colour and keep aside.

Heat oil and add the fried onions, garlic and ginger paste, turmeric powder, coriander powder, red chilli powder and salt. Add a little water and fry for a few minutes till the oil separates. Now add the mincemeat and stir till the water it releases evaporates. Cook on medium flame for about 10 to 15 minutes till mincemeat is half done. Add half a cup of water so that the meat does not burn. Now add whole green chillies, raw onions, raw green mango and fried karela. Cover and cook on low flame till the mincemeat is done. Garnish with fresh mint leaves.

Qeema Bharey Karela – Bitter Gourd with Mince Stuffing

1 kg bitter gourd

1 kg mincemeat

Prepare the mincemeat with the kacha aam qeema recipe. Meanwhile, scrape the outer part of the karela and soak in salted water for half-an-hour. Slit the karela in the middle, remove the seeds. Once the mincemeat is almost done, stuff the karela with it and wrap a thread all around. Ideally, the karelas are sewn with a needle and thread. Heat a little oil, and leave the karela for 15 to 20 minutes on low flame till done. Flip the karela around once or twice to ensure that all sides are evenly browned.

Kacha Aam Qeema – Green Mango Mince

1 kg mincemeat
2 medium-sized onions, golden fried
4 medium-sized raw onions, finely sliced
1 medium-sized raw green mango, peeled and grated
1 tsp red chilli powder
2 tsp garlic paste
1½ tsp ginger paste
½ tsp turmeric powder
2 green chillies, whole
2 tsp coriander powder
½ cup oil
Salt to taste

Qeema cooked with just raw green mango is delicious and has a unique tangy taste. It is cooked in much the same way as karela qeema. However, I will give the recipe lest you get confused.

Heat oil and add fried onions along with garlic and ginger paste, turmeric powder, coriander powder, red chilli powder and salt. Add a little water and fry for few minutes till the oil separates. Now add mincemeat and fry till the water it releases evaporates. Cook on medium flame for about 15 to 20 minutes till half done. Add a little water to ensure that the mincemeat does not burn. Now add green chillies, raw green mango, and raw onions to the meat and cook on low flame till done. Garnish with fresh mint leaves.

Chana Dal Karela – Lentil with Bitter Gourd

200-250 gm chana dal

½ kg karela

2 medium-sized onions, finely chopped

1 tsp Nigella seeds (kalonji)

2 tsp fennel seeds (saunf)

1 tsp red chilli powder

2 green chillies, chopped

1 small raw green mango, peeled, grated or chopped finely

¼ cup oil

Salt to taste

A pinch turmeric powder

Soak the dal for an hour or so. Scrape the karela and remove the seeds. Soak them in water with a little salt to get rid of the bitterness. Then cut the karela into small pieces. Pour the oil in a cooking utensil and add all the ingredients with about two cups of water. The water level should not be too much above the dal. Cook on high flame till the water boils and then lower the flame. Keep covered and cook for 15 to 20 minutes till both the dal and karela are done. The dal should remain whole and dry. It is an art to get the consistency right and this comes with a little practice. Garnish with fresh or dry mint leaves.

Summer Sweet Dishes

Aam Pulao – Mango Rice

½ kg basmati rice

750 gm ripe mangoes

250 gm khoya

6 green cardamoms

¼ cup desi ghee

2 cups sugar or to taste

Khoya is thickened milk and sold at halwai shops. It is used in several
Indian sweets. Many popular mithais such as barfi and milkcake are
made with khoya. In summer, when friends and relatives send barfi
or milkcake, I usually make mango or pineapple pulao with it. If
using mithai, the quantity of sugar used should be reduced. Any
variety of mangoes can be used to make aam pulao, but it tastes best
with the fragrant alphonso, rataul and sarauli mangoes.

Soak the basmati rice in water for about 45 minutes. Cook the rice till it is almost done and there is no water left. Handcrush or grate the khoya and fry lightly to a golden colour. No ghee is needed for khoya releases ghee. Peel the mangoes and cut them into one or two inch pieces.

Now spread a layer of rice in another cooking utensil. Add mango over the rice and sprinkle it with khoya and then sugar. Make one or two more such layers.

Heat desi ghee in a separate pan and add the crushed cardamoms to it. Fry for a minute and then pour the ghee over the rice and mango layers. Cover and leave to simmer for 10 to 15 minutes on low flame till the rice is done. Do not stir as the rice grains should remain whole.

Anannaas Pulao – Pineapple Rice

½ kg basmati rice

750 gm pineapple

250 gm khoya

6 green cardamoms

¼ cup desi ghee

2 cups sugar or to taste

Anannaas pulao is prepared the same way as mango pulao. Just replace the mango with pineapple.

Andarsey ki goliyan

Pakoras, a monsoon favourite

Monsoon

Monsoon in Delhi has forever been associated with romance, swinging from trees, kite flying and picnics. For Dilliwalas, visiting Mehrauli's open spaces for picnics or for a few days during the monsoons is an old tradition. Amma told us stories of how families would travel in camel drawn carriages to Mehrauli. These carriages were carpeted and cushioned. Families began their journey at night and reached their destination the next morning. The sexes were segregated in different carriages, the zenana and mardana. Much like modern farmhouses today, many rich families in yesteryears owned houses in Mehrauli. They extended invitations to friends and relatives to stay in their homes. These retreats were stocked with kitchen provisions for the guests. The Chunnamals, whose famous haveli still stands in Chandni Chowk, were among those families who had a summer home in Mehrauli.

Daddy often recalls his trips to Mehrauli when four or five families travelled together. They hired camel carriages from the stand near Lahori Gate, where the Shradhanand market is today Some families travelled in lorries that provided for intercity travel. Other modes of transport in the old city were horse-drawn tongas and trams. Lorries can be described as a cruder version of today's buses. They were higher, and getting inside was not easy. Although they had seats, they had a door at the back, which the conductor opened to allow access into the lorry. Passengers had to place one leg inside the lorry and jump in. Buses were introduced in Delhi after India attained freedom.

Abba had rented a home in Mehrauli for some years to help his wife regain her health. Amma had been unwell and the hakim advised the fresh air of Mehruali. Those days my father travelled daily from Mehrauli to his school in the old city in a lorry.

Ammi has childhood memories of picnics in the monsoon amongst the ruins of Hauz Khas. Delhi's various monuments once made for wonderful picnic spots. Ammi recounts lazing with friends inside the arches of the monuments as rain lashed the area. When the showers stopped, the girls dyed colourful dupattas, long scarves, sprinkled with silvery abrak. These dupattas were exchanged as friendship tokens, similar to the friendship bands exchanged by youngsters these days.

In the tradition of Amma and Ammi, I too tell my son monsoon stories. With the arrival of the first showers, I remember Amma preparing for a family picnic to Mehrauli. Stoves, cooking cauldrons, food items, gramophone, records, ropes and other requirements were stacked in one corner of the house. Amma and Apa Saeeda made monsoon specialties such as dal bhari roti, that is, roti with dal stuffing, and hari mirch ka qeema, mincemeat cooked with large green chillies.

We drove in our cherry red Dodge convertible car that had a sunroof, which could be drawn fully open. Although meant for seating five, at least ten of us kids would somehow manage to sit inside the car.

On reaching Mehrauli and finding the ideal picnic spot, the elders helped us make *jhoola*, swings, on the trees. We carried the ropes and blocks of wood from home. We sang songs while swinging from the tree branches. Sprawled out on durries amidst the green landscape, the elders played film songs on a gramophone. We looked for khirni trees to pluck the small yellow coloured fruit. Mehrauli also had plenty of gondni, an orange berry-like fruit, and ber bushes. We relished these delights and carried some of the fruit home.

Amma busied herself supervising the food and frying of pakora and gul gule, made with wheat and sugar. Mangoes were cooled in iron tubs full of ice. Mango-eating competitions were held. The one who managed to eat the largest number of mangoes won. We never stayed overnight in Mehrauli, that tradition ended with the Partition.

Eating and distributing suhaal, a mithai, amongst families and friends was a monsoon tradition. Andarsey ki goliyan, small round fried cookies made with rice flour and sprinkled with sesame seeds, is another monsoon specialty. Come the monsoon, I send someone to the old city to get us these delights.

Dilliwalas remain choosy about their mangoes. We don't eat early croppers and prefer to wait for varieties such as dussehri, langra, sarauli, chausa and rataul. Abba loved rataul, preferring it to alphonso, and delighted in distributing them to friends. He had a small contribution in taking rataul to Pakistan. On a train trip to Pakistan during the year 1948, he carried 150 saplings of rataul for friends.

Rataul originally comes from the district of Rataul near Baghpat in Uttar Pradesh. Apparently Anwar, one of the brothers who owned a rataul orchard, migrated to Pakistan. He began growing rataul mangoes in Pakistan that came to be known as anwar rataul. It now grows there in abundance and is one of their best mangoes. In Delhi, this variety is no longer easily available, and one has to request fruit sellers to organize some boxes.

At Shama Kothi, mangoes came in tons of kilos. These were left in a store room to mature. *Aam ki paal*, was the phrase used for this method of storing. Amma checked the lot daily, handpicking the mangoes that had ripened organically. Nowadays mangoes are mostly matured with the use of chemicals that reduce the flavour and taste.

Heaps of mangoes were placed in iron tubs or buckets with ice for a few hours before consumption. Amma said that this neutralized the garam taseer of the mangoes. On my mother's insistence, I still place mangoes in a bucket of water for a few hours before stacking them in the fridge.

When returning from boarding school for our summer holidays, one of the things we looked forward to was mangoes. Amma made jugs of hand-beaten *aamdoodh*, mango shake, each morning and sent it to our bedrooms. She used sarauli mangoes, best for mango shake. Sarauli mangoes are also perfect for making fresh mango chutney.

As a young girl, I loved the small yellow safeda mangoes that are fibreless and can be sucked. I always made such a mess that Ammi regularly dunked me in the bathtub with loads of safeda. Agreed that sucking mangoes is an activity not conducive to table manners, but it's difficult to forgive Ammi for this one! Much like the rataul and sarauli varieties, safeda mangoes are not commonly available. These are not to be confused with banganapalli mangoes from southern India often sold as safeda in Delhi.

In Delhi, the arrival of the monsoon is celebrated with pakora and tea. Hari mirch ka qeema with besani roti is another monsoon must. It is served with fresh mango chutney.

Kadhi is made often during the rains, and so are other besan dishes such as khandviyan, that are made in a batter that is left to set and later cut into diamond shapes. These are then cooked in a gravy made with curd, onion and masala. Khandviyan are tricky and need some practice to get right. Although I watched Apa Saeeda and Amma making these during my childhood, I don't know how to make them.

Hari Mirch Qeema – Green Chilli Mince

10-12 long, thick green chillies
½ kg mincemeat
200 gm curd, lightly beaten
2 tsp coriander powder
¼ tsp turmeric powder
1 tsp garlic paste
¾ tsp ginger paste
4-5 medium-sized onions, golden fried
½ tsp red chilli powder
½ cup oil
Salt to taste

Slice half of the green chillies into two or three pieces and leave the other half whole. Keep these aside.

Heat oil and add the onions along with garlic and ginger paste, coriander powder, chilli powder and salt. Fry for a minute or two and then add the mincemeat. Once the water released by the mince has dried and the oil separates, add a cup of water to ensure that the mincemeat does not burn. When it is half done, add all the green chillies. After 5–10 minutes add the curd. Leave on low flame till done and dry the excess water if any. Garnish with shredded ginger strips.

Shimla Mirch Qeema – Green Capsicum Mince

½ kg capsicum
½ kg mincemeat

Prepare shimla mirch qeema with the same recipe as for hari mirch qeema. Simply replace the large green chillies with capsicums cut into one inch pieces. Garinsh with shredded ginger strips.

Dal Bhari Roti

¼ kilo chana dal
2–3 onions, finely chopped
¼ tsp turmeric powder
½ tsp red chilli powder
Green chillies, finely chopped
Mint leaves, finely chopped
Salt to taste

Boil the dal with a little salt and turmeric. Add just enough water to let the dal remain whole. Be careful not to make it watery. Then mash the dal, add onions, chilli powder and mint leaves to the dal and stuff the roti with this mixture. The easiest way is to make two rotis, layer the stuffing on one and place the other over it. Prepare these like a regular parantha on a flat tawa. The roti is best enjoyed with fresh mango chutney and hari mirch qeema.

Aam Chutney – Fresh Mango Chutney

3 ripe mangoes, peeled and pulped
¼ tsp red chilli powder
½ tsp crushed cumin seeds
1 medium-sized onion, finely chopped
1 green chilli, finely chopped
Few mint leaves, chopped
Few drops of lemon juice (optional)
Salt to taste

Mango chutney is delicious, specially when made with sarauli mango. Since these are not always available, take any good quality mango. Put the pulp in a bowl and add all the remaining ingredients. Aam chutney tastes wonderful with besani roti.

Besani Roti

250 gm gram flour
250 gm wheat flour
1 tsp desi ghee
1 tsp fennel seeds
1 tbsp coriander seeds, whole
½ tsp Nigella seeds (kalonji)
½ cup curd
2 tsp dried mint leaves
3-4 tbsp desi ghee
Salt to taste

The best method to make besani roti is to use wheat and gram flour in equal measure. Use as much curd as needed to prepare the dough. Add desi ghee at the time of kneading. Add the remaining ingredients to the prepared dough and make as parantha. Line the tava with a little desi ghee while making the roti.

Kadhi

Kadhi prepared in our family looks and tastes quite different from the kadhi that I have had elsewhere. We make it spicier and the phulki is large and flat, as opposed to the small, round phulki that is more common.

Phulki

250 gm gram flour
1 medium-sized onion, finely chopped
1 green chilli, finely chopped
¼ tsp Nigella seeds (kalonji)
1 tsp garlic paste

½ tsp red chilli powder

½ tsp baking soda

½ tsp baking powder

1 tbsp coriander seeds, crushed

1 tsp cumin seeds, roasted and crushed

2 cups oil for frying

Salt to taste

Gravy

1 cup gram flour

300–350 gm curd

1 tsp red chilli powder

½ tsp turmeric powder

¼ tsp Nigella seeds (kalonji)

2 medium-sized onions, finely chopped

Salt to taste

Bhagar

10–12 curry leaves (kadhi pata)

6–8 red chillies, whole

¼ cup oil

2 onions, golden fried

Mix the ingredients of the phulki with enough water to make a thick batter. Drop about a tablespoon of the batter by hand in boiling oil. Keep the phulki aside.

Now prepare the gravy for the kadhi. Mix the ingredients for the gravy with 4 cups of water and keep stirring on low flame for about half-an-hour. When it turns thick and is done, add the phulki to the gravy.

For the topping, heat oil in a separate pan and add onions, curry leaves and red chillies. Toss around for a minute before pouring it over the kadhi. Garnish with dried mint leaves.

Kadhi is served with cumin rice. I add a little salt and a spoonful of cumin seeds are fried in a tablespoon or two of oil before adding the rice with water and leaving it to cook.

Sunset - Iftaar time
Photo: Vaseem Ahmed Dehlvi

An iftaar dastarkhwan at my home
Photo: Debbasish Das

Ramzan

As children, we looked forward to Ramzan. We woke up in the early hours of the morning to join the elders for *sehri*, the pre-dawn meal. Similar to the 'midnight feasts' we had at boarding school, these meals seemed exciting. To inculcate the practice of fasting, children were encouraged to observe *ek daad ka roza*, which meant eating carefully through the day from one side of the mouth.

On sighting the sliver of the Ramzan moon, special delicacies from well-known shops of the old city filled the kitchen. These included khajla, pheniyan and unsweetened jalebi, all made with desi ghee. These were soaked in milk a few hours before sehri, after which the fasting hours began.

On the eve of Ramzan, the table in the dining room at home was pushed to one side. A dari chandni, a cotton underlay with a thick sheet covering was put in its place. Just before iftaar time, a dastarkhwan was placed on the chandni and all the family members would sit around this with heads covered, hands folded in prayer. The old, black, heavy telephone which had a long cord was carried to the dining area and we waited for it to ring. A caller would inform us 'roza khol lijiye,' time to end the fast.

This pattern continued well beyond my childhood. I still have no knowledge of the identity of the caller. I presume it was a family acquaintance who lived near Jama Masjid or somewhere in Old Delhi where sirens and gola, sound cannon, are still heard at iftaar time.

After this phone call, we kids went around screaming 'roza khol lo.' This was to inform our staff and their families. We had hung a broken piece of a railway track on a roadside tree beside the staff quarters. We raced against each other to strike it loudly a few times with the help of an iron rod.

In Abba's time, and for many years after, food was distributed in large quantities during the month of Ramzan. For this purpose, each evening a large degh of aloo salan along with bundles of khamiri roti arrived from the old city. Aware of this routine, many friends came home specially to partake of this specialty. My old friend Jameela Apa, a cousin of Ismat Chughtai, would say, 'Allah miyan wala salan khila do,' feed me with God's food.

During the rebellion phase of my teenage years, I confess I did not look forward to Ramzan for it meant adherence to a strict code of conduct. The radio was locked and the television was veiled with a cloth. We were told that the devil is locked and chained during Ramzan. Going to parties or a movie was out of the question. We were almost forced to engage in fast and ritual prayer. If not fasting, we still pretended to and ate discreetly behind closed doors. Amma said it was improper to eat in front of those who were fasting. The Ramzan routine then seemed like a tedious set of rules. I almost began to look forward to getting sick, using even the slightest toothache as an excuse to legitimately escape fasting!

Dahi Badey

Be it for iftaar, high tea or a dinner party, dahi badey are frequently served on the tables of Dilliwalas. Our dahi badey differ from the dahi vadas that are available in restaurants and chaat shops. We make dahi badey round and small whereas vadas are flatter and slightly larger.

Some Dilliwalas make dahi badey with just split green gram, dhuli moong dal, while some mix it with split black gram, urad dal, also called safed maash. Like most in my family, I use a mixture of both these dal. The measure below should make at least 20 to 25 lemon-sized dahi badey.

¼ cup urad dal (safed maash)

¼ cup dhuli moong dal

¼ tsp baking soda

¼ tsp baking powder

½ tsp salt

A good way to ensure that the dahi badey are soft is to soak both dals together overnight or at least for a few hours. The second step is to blend them to a thick paste in a mixer. Do not use extra water to blend as it will turn too watery. There is a trick to making the perfect dahi badey. After blending dal in the mixer, continue to whisk the mixture with a regular or electric eggbeater till it almost doubles.

Add salt, baking soda and baking powder to the whisked batter. Drop a tablespoon from the batter into piping hot oil. Flip the badey around and deep fry them till they acquire a golden hue. Place them on paper towels to soak excess oil.

Just before serving, soak the badey in lukewarm water for a few minutes. Squeeze the badey softly to drain out water. Now, take beaten curd and add a little salt to it. You could also add a teaspoon of sugar. Now add the badey to the curd. Sprinkle the dish with chaat masala. I add a sprinkling of red chilli powder to give it an appetizing colour and garnish with fresh chopped coriander leaves.

Chaat Masala

By themselves, dahi badey are bland and need a sprinkling of a tasty masala. Most readymade chaat masalas are not up to the mark. It is better to make the masala at home. During the good old days of Shama Kothi, the chaat masala came from a woman who lived in Ballimaran. She was referred to as Chotey ki Ma, and the masala came to be called budihya ka masala. Before the old woman died, she gave the secret formula to her daughter-in-law. The masala continued to come home for many years until the texture and quality dropped. Apparently, the daughter-in-law began to use a mixer instead of hand-pounding the masalas. This changed the

coarse texture of the masala to a fine powder. At some point in our
lives, the masala disappeared from our table. My hunt for the perfect
chaat masala continues. My cousin Ainee gave me this masala recipe,
which is the closest to the one made by Chotey ki Ma.

125-150 gm red chillies (whole)
125 gm coriander seeds (whole)
75 gm cumin seeds
A few tsps of black salt (kala namak)

Roast the red chillies lightly over a tava. Don't let them turn too
dark. Roast the coriander seeds and cumin seeds separately. Grind
all three ingredients together in a mixer and add kala namak. Do
not grind to a fine powder, leave the masala a little coarse. If you
find it too spicy, then roast some more cumin seeds and coriander
seeds and add to the mixture in equal proportion.

Qalmi Badey

1 cup chana dal, soaked overnight
1 medium-sized onion, finely chopped
6 peppercorns, coarsely ground
1 tsp coarse red chilli powder (kutti lal mirch)
Salt to taste
Oil for frying

Drain the water from the soaked dal. Ideally, the dal should be
ground on a sil. If grinding in the mixer, use just a few drops of
water. Add the chilli powder, onion, peppercorns and salt to the dal.
Make large balls with it, almost the size of a tennis ball and deep-fry
them to a golden brown colour. Once cooled, slice them into ¼"
pieces and deep fry again to a dark brown. Drain excess oil on a
paper towel and sprinkle the badey with a little chaat masala. Serve
with fresh green chutney.

Qeemay ki Goliyan – Mince Pakora

250 gm mincemeat
½ cup gram flour (besan)
2 green chillies, finely chopped
1 medium-sized onion, finely chopped
1 tbsp coriander seeds, lightly crushed
1 tsp garlic paste
½ tsp garam masala
½ tsp baking soda
½ tsp red chilli powder
Few fresh coriander leaves, chopped
Salt to taste
Oil for frying

Mix the mincemeat with all the ingredients except for the baking soda and marinate for an hour or two. Just before frying, add the

Khajla being sold in the old city
Photo: Mayank Austen Soofi

Pheniyan being fried for Ramzan in Ballimaran
Photo: Vaseem Ahmed Dehlvi

baking soda. Make balls, smaller than a lemon, and deep fry. Place
on a paper towel to drain excess oil. Serve with fresh green chutney.

Kachalu – Fruit Chaat

Bananas

Guavas

Papaya

Apples

Pineapple

Oranges

Other fruits

Kachalu is what we Dilliwalas call our version of fruit chaat. Kachalu
always has bananas and papaya as they are available all through the
year. Following the lunar calendar, Ramzan moves through the
seasons. So, whichever seasonal fruit is available goes into kachalu;
be it pineapple, grapes, guavas, apples, mangoes, oranges or pears.
The fruits are cut into small pieces and mixed together with lime
juice, a little sugar and chaat masala. Kachalu is mostly reserved for
Ramzan.

Pakoras for iftaar

Dry Chana Dal – Lentil Snack

250 gm chana dal, boiled
4 medium-sized onions, finely chopped
½-1 tsp red chilli powder
5-6 green chillies, finely chopped
Fresh coriander leaves, chopped
Lime juice
Chaat masala
Salt to taste

Chana dal is ideally soaked in water for a few hours before cooking. If not, use a pressure cooker for one whistle. Boil dal in water with red chilli powder and salt. Do not add too much water as the dal should be dry and remain whole. When it is cooked, add onions, coriander leaves, green chillies, lime juice and chaat masala.

Sevaiyan being sold in the old city

Eid

Eid ul Fitr is the major annual Muslim festival. The excitement at Shama Kothi on *chaand raat,* the night before Eid, is a treasured childhood memory. At sunset, we rushed to the terrace to sight the Eid moon. On sighting we greeted each other with *'chand mubarak'* and folded our hands in prayer while gazing at the new moon. When it could not be seen, we waited patiently for the formal announcement from Jama Masjid.

The elders then busied themselves planning the Eid feast. We girls became occupied with *choori mehndi,* bangles and henna. The iconic Babu Churiwala's shop in Ballimaran was our favourite store for bangles. An engaging old man, the talkative Babu spoke in the typical old city dialect and seemed to know everyone by name! We also bought new footwear from Ballimaran.

On returning from the crowded and colourful Eid bazaar, Apa Saeeda applied mehndi on our hands. She made simple patterns, mostly something called *bataq.* This swan-like pattern was formed by placing a thick henna strip in the middle of the palm and then closing the fist. Intricate henna patterns became popular decades later. While we moved around with our hands closed, Apa Saeeda would sew the *gota,* bling edgings, on our clothes. Wearing new clothes and new footwear are Eid traditions. Even today, the old city shops selling clothes, footwear and food remain open almost all through chaand raat.

On Eid, children are given *Eidi,* gift money, from the elders. In the morning, while the women of the house scrambled around getting lunch ready, we kids went about collecting Eidi. Family elders usually kept envelopes filled with crisp new notes ready. Since ours was a joint family, we collected quite a lot of money. We went to the neighbourhood stall to buy chocolates and flavoured milk from Keventers, the then famous dairy product factory which was close by.

The next day we visited relatives who lived in other areas. At Shama Kothi, there were long queues to collect Eidi. Workers from the telephone, post and telegraph department, tailors, office staff and others lined up at the porch. Abba made sure that no one went away empty handed.

In those days, Eid was an elaborate affair with dozens of guests coming in and out. The elders had their friends visiting and we had ours, so much so that Eid lunch would almost turn into dinner. With the ancestral home gone, Eid is no longer the same. My cousins now live in different corners of the city. Given the distances and traffic, we rarely get to meet. We message or greet one another on the phone, but it's just not the same as *gale milna*, that special Eid hug.

Barring Ammi and Daddy, most of the elders who gave me Eidi have passed on to the next world. Life comes full circle and now it is mostly me giving Eidi. I maintain the family tradition of keeping an open house on Eid. My parents, brothers, nephews and countless friends come over for lunch. Although I live in a flat, we manage to host a fairly largle number of guests.

Sabir, whom I have trained over the years, helps in the cooking. We begin our preparations a day earlier and manage to serve four or five main dishes. It's an informal lunch, with guests dropping in all through the day. Since cooking begins at seven in the morning, I feel totally exhausted by the evening. Sometimes, I go to a friend's home for Eid dinner, but am usually too tired to venture out anywhere.

Sevaiyan

Eid ul Fitr is associated with sevaiyan, which is prepared early morning in large quantities. It's one of the few dishes that my mother makes really well and cooks it for us every Eid. It is prepared in many ways. A popular dry variety of sevaiyan is called Muzafar. We mostly make sevaiyan in milk that is called sheer khurma.

200-250 gm sevaiyan
2 litre milk
100 gm sweetened condensed milk (optional)
5-6 green cardamoms
4 tbsp desi ghee
½ tsp kewra water
1 cup sugar or to taste
A few almonds, finely sliced
A few pistachios, finely sliced

A few raisins

Dried dates, finely sliced (chuarey)

A little desiccated coconut

Few strands of saffron soaked in milk (optional)

Heat milk to a boiling point and then lower the flame. Cook the milk till it reduces to almost half the original quantity. Meanwhile, heat desi ghee and add crushed cardamoms and allow them to crackle. Now handcrush the sevaiyan into tiny pieces. Add these to the ghee and keep stirring for a few minutes. Make sure that the flame is kept at a minimum so the sevaiyan don't burn. They should be slightly browned. Then add sevaiyan to the milk and leave uncovered on low flame for almost an hour.

When the sevaiyan are almost done, add sugar. Cook for another 5 to 10 minutes till it thickens to the right consistency. If you add the sugar earlier, the sevaiyan may burn. Now add kewra water and if you are using saffron, this is the time to add it.

Allow the sevaiyan to cool before adding the condensed milk. Lastly, add raisins, dates, slivers of almond, pistachios and dessicated coconut. Serve hot or cold, depending on the season.

Condensed milk is not used in traditional recipes, but it's a good trick that works. If not adding sweetened condensed milk, then increase the quantity of sugar.

Before slicing the almonds, it is best to soak them overnight so they peel easily. Chuarey are also best soaked overnight so they can be easily sliced. We call these slivers of almonds and other dried fruits *havaiyaan*.

Eid al Azha

Eid al Azha is popularly known as Baqra Eid. At Shama Kothi, a truckload of about twenty goats would arrive two or three days before Eid. The healthiest goat was sacrificed for the sake of Prophet Muhammad ﷺ. There was one sacrificial goat for every adult member of the house and a few on behalf of some departed elders.

As soon as the goats arrived, we kids chose a goat each to befriend. We fed the goats and played with them in the gardens. These goats grazed in a large *kucha* part of the house near the kitchen. The *qurbani*, sacrifice, took place in this area which was mostly used for cooking during weddings. Professional cooks were hired and their requirements provided to them. The tandoor would be dug in this ground so fresh roti could be made. The open area had rows of papaya trees. These are commonly planted in Muslim homes as papaya is used for marinating meat.

On Eid morning, the butchers arrived early, just as the men of the house returned from Idgah, where the congregational prayer is held. My father, uncles, brother and cousin brothers would do the qurbani, *churi pherna*, as it is called. They put the knife to the jugular of the goat, and left the rest to the butcher as is the custom. The sacrifice can be done over three days. With the vast number of goats, it was not possible to sacrifice them in a single day. The meat had to be distributed, which was a time-consuming process. The kitchen and its surrounding areas were filled with meat for those three days. With help from the staff, my mother and aunts made packets of meat for distribution. Traditionally, one-third of the sacrificial meat is given to the poor, one-third to friends and relatives and the family keeps the remaining portion.

As children, we were disturbed by the unsettling sight of the goats being slaughtered. I often locked myself in my room. Once a few school friends who visited me on Eid al Azha became upset by the sacrificial scenes. From then on, I never invited any friends on this Eid! Now that I live in a flat, it is just not possible to have qurbani at home, so the sacrifice is done elsewhere.

As a young girl, the idea of meals with sacrificial meat bothered me. However, the elders insisted that one should at least taste a small portion from it as partaking from the qurbani meat is a sunnah, tradition of Prophet Muhammad ﷺ. Apa Saeeda and the elders would remind us of Prophet Abraham's story.

Eid al Azha marks the culmination of the Hajj pilgrimage. It is the day that Muslims around the world join the millions of pilgrims in their joy and thanksgiving to Allah. Hajj, which is making the pilgrimage to the House of Allah in Mecca if one is able, is one of the five pillars of Islam. According to Islamic doctrine, Prophet Adam built the Kaaba at Mecca. It is believed that the Kaaba was damaged in floods during the time of Prophet Noah. Later, the Kaaba was rebuilt by Prophet Abraham.

When Prophet Abraham completed the reconstruction of the Kaaba, he had a dream where God asked him to sacrifice Ishmael, his son. The Quran affirms the dreams of Prophets to be true. On hearing God's command, Ishmael did not flinch and told his father that he was willing to be sacrificed. As Abraham readied for the ultimate sacrifice and placed a knife on his son, Allah called to him: 'O Abraham, you have fulfilled the dream! Thus, do We reward the good doers! That was a clear test.' A ram was sent down from heaven to be sacrificed instead of Ishmael.

It is this spirit of complete submission to God that is celebrated on Eid al Azha. Muslims who can afford it sacrifice a sheep, goat or other prescribed animals. The Quran says, 'It is not their meat nor their blood that reaches Allah; it is your piety that reaches Him.'

At Shama Kothi, Eid al Azha was usually a family affair. Lunch always included mutton stew, yakhni pulao and *kaleji*, liver. Since sacrificial meat is from healthier and older goats, it takes longer than tender mutton to cook. This meat has a high content of fat, which is why very little or no oil is required.

Raan Musallam is an Eid must, but since it requires at least two days of marinating, it is mostly served on the third day. Eid festivities typically last for three days. Ameena Auntie always made the raan and this is her recipe. If you want the whole leg of goat, I suggest placing a prior request with the meat shop.

Raan Musallam

1½–2 kg raan
2–3 lemons
6–8 cloves
½ cup oil
Salt and pepper to taste

Use a fork or sharp knife to prick the leg all over. You could also make small incisions for the marination to go deep. Marinate with lemon juice, salt and pepper. Refrigerate for two days.

Use a large cooking utensil that takes the whole leg comfortably. Heat oil and add cloves. After a minute or two, add the raan and leave on low flame for about an hour till the meat is tender. Add a little water if required to keep it from burning. Serve with a carving knife. We called this hunter meat. Sandwiches made with strips of the raan are delicious.

Raan Musallam Masala

1½–2 kg raan
2–3 lemons
1 kg curd
4 whole kachri, crushed or 2 tsp kachri powder
250–300 gm raw papaya, peeled and pulped
2 tsp garlic paste
6–8 cloves

1½-2 tsp red chilli powder

½ cup oil

1-2 tsp black pepper, freshly ground

Salt to taste

Use a fork or sharp knife to make small incisions on the raan. To make it more manageable, you could make a deep cut on the bend of the leg and fold it.

Marinate the raan with salt, kachri, pepper, red chilli powder and lemon juice. Refrigerate for a day or two. A few hours before cooking, marinate the raan again with curd, garlic and papaya.

Heat oil and add cloves. Now place the raan in a large utensil that accommodates it and leave on low flame for about an hour till done. Flip the raan once to ensure even browning. If required, add a little water to keep the raan from burning. The curd and other spices form a little masala, so spread it around the raan in the serving platter.

Kaleji – Liver Curry

Kaleji for lunch is another Eid al Azha tradition, specially since it cooks quickly. This is prepared with the basic salan recipe. Generally, 3 to 4 teaspoon of dried kasuri methi leaves are added to the kaleji a few minutes before turning off the flame.

Fried Mutton Chops

1 kg mutton chops

2 tsp cumin seeds, crushed

2 tsp garlic paste

1 tsp red chilli powder

2 beaten eggs

Breadcrumbs

Oil for frying

Salt to taste

Marinate the mutton chops with the cumin, salt, chilli powder, and garlic paste for a few hours. Heat oil, add marinated chops and leave on low flame for 30 to 35 minutes till they are almost done. If needed, add a little water so that the chops don't burn. Now, dip the chops in beaten eggs, coat with breadcrumbs and deep fry. Serve with fresh green chutney or tomato ketchup.

Masala Chops with Thick Gravy

1 kg mutton chops

Marination

4 kachri or 2 tsp kachri powder

250 gm curd

2 medium-sized onion, minced

1 tsp red chilli powder

½ cup raw papaya, peeled and pulped

4 tbsp oil

Salt to taste

Mix all the ingredients and marinate the mutton chops overnight or for at least 4 to 6 hours. Heat oil and cook the chops on low flame till they are tender. Masala chops are served with roti.

Meetha – Sweet Dishes

Halwas were rarely cooked at home, they mostly came from reputed shops. In winter, we often had homemade andey ka halwa. Sometimes Apa Saeeda made harira with rava. She added some milk so it became more like a porridge. Amongst the sweet dishes made at home were firni, kheer, shahi tukdey and sevaiyan.

Firni and Kheer

Firni and kheer are similar, except for the texture. In firni the rice is danedar whereas kheer is made with whole rice. Kheer is thicker and sets well after cooking whereas firni does not.

Kheer

2 litre milk
½ cup basmati rice, preferably broken
4-6 cardamoms crushed
10-12 almonds, peeled and finely sliced (optional)
10-12 pistachios, finely sliced (optional)
1½ cup sugar or to taste
½ tsp kewra water
Few strands of saffron (optional)
Edible silver leaves (optional)

Kheer is best made with broken basmati rice. Soak it for 35 to 45 minutes. If using regular basmati rice, then lightly handcrush it after soaking it. Meanwhile, bring the milk to boil and then lower the flame to the minimum. Now add the rice and continue cooking uncovered for almost an hour till the milk reduces to less than half. Keep stirring so that no lumps are not formed. After the rice is completely cooked, add sugar and keep stirring till you have the right consistency. If you wish to add saffron, now is the time to add it. Soak the saffron in a tablespoon of warm milk and add to kheer. Lastly, add kewra water just before turning off the flame.

Pour kheer into a serving bowl or in clay bowls and leave to set. Garnish with *chandi key warq*, edible silver leaves, and slivers of almond and pistachio.

Shahi Tukda – Royal Bread Pudding

4 bread slices, white

1 litre milk

¼ tsp kewra

4 green cardamoms, crushed or powdered

½ cup desi ghee

½ cup sugar or to taste

Few strands of saffron (optional)

Saffron colouring

Sliced almonds and pistachios (optional)

Edible silver leaves (optional)

Slice the bread pieces in the middle into halves. You can remove the crust but it is not necessary. Deep fry the slices to golden brown and keep aside.

Add cardamoms to milk and put it to boil. Ideally use a wide utensil for the milk so that when bread slices are added later, they spread nicely. Reduce the milk to almost half so it thickens. Add the sugar to the milk and let it dissolve. Add saffron colouring or saffron to the milk. Now add fried bread slices to the milk and leave on low flame for around 15 to 20 minutes. The bread slices will absorb all the milk. Do not use a spoon and do not cover the utensil as the slices will break. Just turn the utensil around a bit. Add kewra just before turning off the flame.

Take the slices out with a large flat spoon and place on the serving platter. Garnish with pistachio and almond slivers. Lastly, to make the dish look royal, dress it with a few edible silver leaves.

Zarda – Flavoured Rice

½ kg sella or basmati rice

8 green cardamoms

8 cloves

½ cup desi ghee

1½-2 cup sugar or to taste

¼ tsp saffron colour powder

1 tsp kewra

2 tbsp curd (optional)

250 gm khoya, grated or handcrushed

Few strands of saffron or saffron colouring (optional)

For zarda, the sella variety of rice is preferred over basmati as the latter breaks easily. I prefer using the fragrant basmati.

If using basmati rice, soak the rice for 45 minutes. Sella rice needs to be soaked for 3 to 4 hours prior to cooking. Boil 5-6 glasses of water with 4 cloves and 4 crushed cardamoms. Add a little saffron colouring to the water. Add rice to the boiling water. Once the rice is completely cooked, strain it and keep it aside. In another saucepan, heat ghee and the remaining cloves and cardamoms. Let them crackle for a minute or two and add the sugar along with half a cup of water to prepare the *chaashni*, sugar syrup. Keep stirring till the sugar dissolves completely and the syrup thickens. You could add a little curd to the syrup as it prevents the rice from turning hard.

Now add the rice to the syrup, mix well and cook uncovered on high flame till the syrup has been absorbed and dried. Add khoya to the rice and cook covered on minimum flame for about 10 to 15 minutes. Add kewra to the rice just before switching of the flame,

When serving, garnish with *murabba,* preserved cherries, almond and pistachio slivers. If you like, add some fried or roasted almonds and cashews. Silver warq placed over zarda gives it the final royal touch.

Pickles and Chutneys

Apart from a few chutneys and achaar that go with specific dishes, Dilliwalas rarely have pickle on their table. Arq-e-nana chutney is enjoyed with haleem, shalgam ka achaar with matar pulao and the lime achaar aids digestion.

Arq-e-Nana Chutney – Sweet Sour Chutney

In Arabic, *arq* means distillate and *nana* means mint. Earlier it was used in making this chutney. Over the years, it has been replaced by glacial ascetic acid, an organic compound with a chemical formula.

½ kg raw green mango, peeled
1-2 tsp Nigella seeds (kalonji)
4-6" ginger piece cut into fine long strips
15-20 small garlic pods, whole
½ tsp red chilli powder
6-8 red chillies, broken into small pieces
1 cup sugar or to taste
100 gm raisins
1 tbsp of glacial ascetic acid
100 gm chaaron maghaz – melon, pumpkin and watermelon
seeds (optional)
A few dates, sliced into strips (chuarey)
Salt to taste

Soak the dried dates for a few hours and cut into fine long strips.
Slice the mango into small, fine 1" strips or grate it. Some prefer
using small, whole pods of garlic. You can use some of it sliced
lengthwise into strips and some whole. Except for sugar and ascetic
acid, boil all other ingredients together in 3-4 glasses of water for 15
to 20 minutes on low flame. Then add sugar and cook for another 5
to 10 minutes. After it cools, add a tablespoon of glacial ascetic acid.
You can refrigerate the chutney and enjoy it with pulaos, haleem
and other dishes.

Neembu Achaar – Lemon Pickle

I remember Amma storing achaar in large *martabaan*, ceramic jars. She would wait for the lemon trees in the garden to bear fruit and then made pickle using just lemons and salt. She had the lemons scraped on a stone slab, and then preserved in lemon juice squeezed from other lemons. Lahori namak, rock salt, was crushed and added to the whole lemons and lemon juice. These were put out in the sun to mature. More rock salt was added to it during the next few following days. The salt preserved the pickle and crusts over the lemons. When we had stomach ailments, Amma gave us a small piece of this lemon pickle for its medicinal purpose. It is said that the older the pickle, the better it becomes.

Ammi recalls that when Amma had once left Delhi on a vacation, she decided to clean the kitchen and pantry thoroughly. On finding the lemon pickle with salt crust all over it, she mistook it for fungus and threw away the pickle. When Amma returned and learnt about the missing pickle, she threw up her hands in despair. She told Ammi that she had thrown away a priceless fifteen-year-old pickle! Making it is rather simple.

12 lemons, whole
12 lemons, juiced
Rock salt (Lahori namak)

It is a tedious job to scrape the lemons on stone, so just use lemons with thin skin. Keep a dozen lemons whole and extract juice from the remaining dozen. Put the whole lemons in a glass jar with the lemon juice and rock salt. Leave this mixture in the sun for a month or so. Keep adding a little salt every second or third day for around a fortnight. When the lemons become soft, your pickle is ready.

Shalgam Pani Achaar – Turnip Water Pickle

1 kg turnips, peeled
3-4 tbsp coarse red chilli powder (kutti lal mirch)
4 tbsp garlic paste
200 gm mustard seeds (rai)
Salt to taste

Chop the turnips into two and then make ½" thick slices. Boil them with 5-6 glasses of water. Turn off the flame after one boil and then strain the turnips. Meanwhile, grind the mustard seeds to a coarse texture in a mixer. Now spread the turnips on a large tray and marinate with mustard powder, red chilli powder, garlic paste and salt. Ideally, the boiled turnip slices should be covered with a muslin cloth and put out in the sun for a day or two. With the air so polluted, I don't do that anymore. I just leave them in the kitchen for a few hours. It is best served with matar pulao.

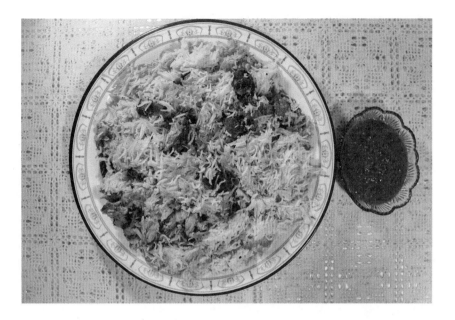

Now boil around a litre of fresh water and let it cool. Put the turnip slices in a glass jar and pour the cooled water over them. Keep the jar in the sun for a week or two as it takes time for the *khataas*, tanginess, to set in. Refrigerating the pickle makes it last for a few months. Shalgam ka achaar is best enjoyed with all varieties of pulaos. This is a healthy, water-based preserve.

Lasan Lal Mirch Chutney – Garlic Red Chilli Chutney

15-20 garlic pods, peeled
6-7 red chillies, whole
¼ onion, chopped
½ tsp cumin seeds
Salt to taste

Grind all the ingredients in a blender. This is a hot, spicy chutney, often served with biryani, shaami kebab and pakora.